Handling
BAD

Handling
BAD

Inside a Cyber Era
Private Investigative Firm

Daniel Robert Weiss

Published by Advantage, Charleston, South Carolina.
Member of Advantage Media Group.

ADVANTAGE is a registered trademark and the Advantage colophon is a trademark of Advantage Media Group, Inc.

Printed in the United States of America.

ISBN: 978-1-59932-591-0
LCCN: 2015950222

This publication is designed to provide accurate and authoritative information in regard to the subject matter covered. It is sold with the understanding that the publisher is not engaged in rendering legal, accounting, or other professional services. If legal advice or other expert assistance is required, the services of a competent professional person should be sought.

Advantage Media Group is proud to be a part of the Tree Neutral® program. Tree Neutral offsets the number of trees consumed in the production and printing of this book by taking proactive steps such as planting trees in direct proportion to the number of trees used to print books. To learn more about Tree Neutral, please visit www.treeneutral.com. To learn more about Advantage's commitment to being a responsible steward of the environment, please visit www.advantagefamily.com/green

Advantage Media Group is a publisher of business, self-improvement, and professional development books and online learning. We help entrepreneurs, business leaders, and professionals share their Stories, Passion, and Knowledge to help others Learn & Grow. Do you have a manuscript or book idea that you would like us to consider for publishing? Please visit advantagefamily.com or call 1.866.775.1696.

The reader should be forewarned that this is an unedited, full adult version of my work. I have made no attempt to simply shock the reader, however, the stories and the content can be shocking. The language is in full color, and if you are easily offended, I suggest you pick up another book.

The stories in this book are based on actual cases. However, material facts, names, and locations have been changed to protect the confidential nature of our work.

DEDICATION

The book is dedicated to three people.

First, to the memory of my late brother, Michael David Weiss, who died in the midst of a crime scene in 1999 at the age of thirty-two. Since I have always had the innate propensity to find meaning and opportunity in even the worst of situations, his murder was a key incident in directing my path to the investigative business. I remember looking at his body and realizing how unprepared I was to deal with such a scene. Leaving it up to the police without having a real advocate on the case inevitably relegated his death to the pile of unsolved murders that clog every major city. I understood in that very second how impactful being that advocate could be for someone, regardless if it was murder, sexual assault, infidelity, or fraud.

I understand how critical rapid and quality investigations are to containing an unfolding crisis. *Time may help to heal pain, but it doesn't make insight on an event any clearer.* Being that person, that firm which can help someone handle a bad situation, became a very clear life purpose for me.

Second, this is dedicated to my father, Leon Weiss, with whom I am fortunate to be able to speak almost daily. Dad is a legendary probate litigator in the old-school city of Cleveland, Ohio. He has always been a great counselor and has listened to me with a patient ear since my early college years. He has been a rock and has always been there for me during good times and bad. Without his help, I would not have been able to be in the profession I am in today. His example has set a high bar that I can only hope I meet with my own children. Few people can rapidly digest my analysis of a situation; he is one of the very few who can not only digest it but also add valuable feedback. One could not ask for a better father. As my late Grandpa Bill said, I am a member of the lucky sperm club.

Third, I dedicate this to my wife, Michelle Weiss. Momma, as she is known, has been my partner since we met when I was eighteen years old at UT Austin. I can define my life as pre- and post-Momma. We raised each other as young adults to actual adults, the latter status having been reached approximately when we turned forty. She has graced me with love and a family that has exceeded anything I could have imagined. I basically would not be if it were not for Michelle—it is that simple. How can you thank someone like that? I can only hope she knows how deeply I love her. I have been a lot of things to her, and I think this book may show the key to me keeping her in my life; I am not boring. She can't help but want to watch the next chapter. All you get to do is read it; I save the live action for the best person—Momma.

ACKNOWLEDGMENTS

The creation of this book was a process born out of my membership in the Entrepreneurs' Organization (EO), a group of business owners that I'm proud to have been a member of for almost two decades. EO has been a very meaningful group for me. It welcomes those afflicted by entrepreneurship, and as a group we work to make our business better for our clients, employees, families, and ourselves.

In this nonprofit group, we share experiences that have changed our business and our personal lives, both for the better and worse. We don't lecture; we simply share experiences.

I listened to a few members talk about writing books and how it transformed their businesses and impacted their lives. I did my best to ignore the calling, since it required a real commitment to get it done. Finally, my internal voice won over, and I decided to jump in.

I thank my team of investigators who put up with me daily and work to deliver the truth to our clients, regardless of how painful the facts are. I simply play a role in the issues we address daily; without them, it would be impossible to perform the work that we provide. The word "team" is often misused and overused … it is not the case at our firm. We work as a team daily.

I was fortunate to have made the connection with Advantage Media Group and their very professional and measured process of getting difficult fish into the boat. I was also most fortunate to have won over a great partner in crime in Jenny Tripp, my editor, who was thick skinned enough to listen to my stories and engage with me at a real level. This book was no easy task, as Jenny had to wade through my recollections of conversations and interviews pertaining to cases. This book would never have made it to print without her help; she performed a true mitzvah. Thank you, Jenny.

TABLE OF CONTENTS

INTRODUCTION

WELCOME TO THE WILD CYBER FRONTIER

These are strange times we live in. The line between the actual and the virtual has never been thinner. The new world of cyberspace and the Internet of Everything has created new opportunities for businesses, consumers, academics, and everyday people. It has also produced new realms to explore for the dark-hearted among us. The world is now flat and digi-dimensional, with new paths being developed by the thousands every second. While we can see all the positives if we look through the Silicon Valley lens, the truth is much more nuanced. The field of potential victims is vast and teeming with opportunity, like a scene from a science-fiction movie: target-rich. The fact is there has never been a better time to be a cybercentric perpetrator. These are Gold Rush days.

The Internet has created a wide-open field where criminals of all stripes—sex offenders, extortionists, pedophiles, and swindlers—can operate freely, without much fear of reprisal and even less fear of law enforcement, whose crime-fighting and investigative methodologies are largely stuck in the last millennium. The bald fact is that ordinary people—and their kids—are just low-hanging fruit, and nobody's guarding the orchard.

Yet most private investigators and local law enforcement agencies don't even have their own computer forensic labs, much less the skills to run them. If you're hacked—if someone decides to steal your industrial secrets, cyberstalk you, or plant kiddie-porn on your computer—chances are good that nobody in local law enforcement will have any idea how to handle your case. And Homeland Security, or the regional shared digital forensic labs, is busy chasing bigger fish.

It's an ever-expanding world, and the Internet has impacted how we live in it as much, if not more, than the invention of the printing press did. More than 80 percent of the information generated today only exists digitally. Increasingly, criminals are using the digital realm to access victims and commit crimes. If you don't have the competence to go after information stored in digital formats as well as analogue formats, you're not getting the full picture—and you're not going to catch them.

We exist to fill this gap. Our tool kit is a combination of traditional detective work with cutting-edge digital investigation. How that works in real-time detective work is the subject of this book. All of these are actual case histories. The names of the people involved have been changed, as have other identifying details, for the victims' protection—but their suffering at the hands of those who targeted them is very real. I think you'll find these accounts eye opening and occasionally painful to read. This is not written to shock. If it does shock you, it is because the cases are filled with the kinds of horror stories only real life can generate.

It's my hope that by writing this book, I can encourage those in the private investigations business and policy makers who impact law enforcement to gain expertise in this largely ignored digital realm in which so much modern crime takes place. I hope, too, that reading these stories may prevent someone out there from falling victim to a similar fate.

CHAPTER ONE

PROFILE OF A PROFILER

M ost private investigators come out of law enforcement, but I took a different path. I was in graduate school in psychology and working as a psychology intern at a maximum-security prison in the Boston area. My work behind "the wall" at Walpole State Prison taught me a lot about the extremes of human nature and criminology in particular. You have to do something fairly serious to end up at Walpole State Prison, so most of the prison is filled with habitual offenders, more familiarly known as "bitches"—mostly blue-collar career criminals, versus the Club Fed where you'd find the Bernard Madoffs and their white-collar friends. This was a male prison, so the guys there were sex offenders, pedophiles, murderers, organized crime enforcers, and rapists—the full gamut of bad.

When a person comes into prison, part of the process is a psychological screening, which was my job. My way of looking beyond the sociological and psychological theory I was studying was nurtured by this experience. You would start each meeting by first looking through the files on these guys. These files, each of which could have filled a drawer, basically covered these individuals' entire lives. Looking through an average file was like reading an illustrated tutorial on the path to criminality; you could see the trail through early juvenile delinquency and torturing animals; to setting fires, minor arrests, and drug pops; then to breaking into cars and gang activity. It was just that predictable and clear. Call it categorizing or stereotyping; it was profiling in its purest state, regardless of how un-politically correct it might sound.

The prison population at Walpole by and large was made up of lifelong career criminals, 85 percent of whom would be back in maximum-security prison within a couple of years of getting out. They used their time inside to add to their skill sets. *We study criminology; they study crime.* A guy who was an expert in armed robbery would become friends with a guy who was an expert in forgery. They literally would train each other; it was the equivalent of an associate's degree, with the ability to get advanced undergraduate degrees in the various esoteric verticals of being a criminal. How do you extort someone? How do you fence stolen office equipment? What are the best techniques for a physical shakedown? What is the best way to avoid motion detectors?

I'd go through the file and I'd read the first person information, and then I'd read the police reports, caseworkers' notes, etc., and then I'd read the associated court cases. I was looking for those multiple-dimension data points about the person. Of course, the last data point about the person was my in-person interview. I'd have read all of the background about this person who'd had, for instance, a lifelong career as a rapist, who'd maybe assaulted a child. I'd look through this stuff and think, *Holy shit, I'm about to meet Jeffrey Dahmer.* And then the guy would come in my office—and almost always, he wasn't what I'd expected. Oftentimes, these guys were disarmingly charming and able to carry on very insightful conversations.

Most of the people I met there fell into three categories. The first kind of guy could have been anyone's risk-taking, kind of wild, shortsighted friend, uncle, or neighbor. He could just be a regular guy, except that he was prone to making bad decisions and had figured out a quicker way to make a living versus the normal social ladders and processes; in other words, an entrepreneur of the pro-fessional criminal class. This category-one type is what you refer to as a straight-up con. A straight con is a breaking and entering guy. He's a drug dealer; he's a mafia enforcer; he's not a rapist, he's not a child molester, and he doesn't beat up elderly people. These guys have standards; they are criminal standards but standards nonetheless.

I'll never forget the conversation I had with one of them who was getting out after doing a five-year bid for selling crack cocaine. Not only was he a crack cocaine dealer, but he had also introduced his underage kids into the narcotics business. He had been doing some work release, making ten dollars an hour, so he was making three dollars an hour more than I was as a graduate student. I said to him, "Hey, man, you're getting out! What are you going to do?"

He looked at me like I was stupid and said, "I'm going to sell drugs." I couldn't believe it; he said, "You're a doctor, that's what you do. I'm a drug dealer, that's what I do."

Aside from the fact that he'd gifted me with a degree I hadn't earned, this was a very clarifying moment because I accepted philo-sophically what he said. I might not like it; I might find it offensive, I might reach all kinds of conclusions about him, but he was telling me something from his behavior. *I look at data points, and I look at real behavioral patterns. You can tell me a lot of things, but I want to see what you do. What you do or did is how I define you, how I profile you.* No matter what I offered him, no matter what educational or vocational programs he had access to, he was a drug dealer—period. He was a true habitual offender—a real bitch. He was simply going to teach the family trade to his kids. It was really no more complex than that.

In my business, I've been in diamond vaults that contain hundreds of millions of dollars of raw diamonds. I've been in cash reserves that would boggle people's minds. I have been invited behind the curtain and worked with the wealthiest people and in the wealthiest businesses. If I wanted to be a criminal, I could. I could do hackings, extortions, everything you can imagine. But I don't. And the reason I don't has nothing to do with my economic status, my race, or anything else; I don't do that, because I'm not a criminal.

The second category was made up of the true deviants, and by that I mean that their behavior was driven by some darkness—maybe a wrinkle in their childhood development or maybe genetics. They weren't motivated by their need to make a living and provide for their families or even to feed a drug addiction; they were motivated by something else. A lot of them were sex offenders, child molesters, or sadistic rapists. This was a mind-blowing experience for me; sometimes you'd read the file and meet the guy, and it was just so evident that he was evil and out of his freaking mind. But occasionally, I'd meet someone and have no idea. That was a real eye-opener for me.

One of the latter was a Harvard student who'd sadistically raped two of his professors. He came into the Psych ER with some kind of bullshit complaint, but as we looked into it, the real problem was that the guys in the cell next to him kept dying and always in the same way—by hanging themselves. How could this be a coincidence? Turned out, the reason they kept dying was this guy was instructing them on autoerotic asphyxiation; he was teaching these guys how to hang themselves while they masturbated, and he would masturbate while they were doing it. However, he would leave out a few key pieces of instruction, so they would asphyxiate. He got off by listening to them die. He just liked coming to talk to the psych interns, and he would use it to see how close we were to catching on to him. I think the process amused him. He was a good example of type two.

Category three included the straight-up mental patients who really had no place in the prison system, in my view; they were usually schizophrenic or suffering some sort of organic mental illness, and prison was a nightmare for them as well as for those who had to deal with them. Everyone talks about locking someone in jail and throwing away the key, but they don't think about the staff that has to deal with these people. I don't know if you've ever seen what it looks like for a mentally stable person to be in twenty-three-hour-a-day lockdown; it's not pretty. However, for the mentally ill, it's far worse, and they don't handle it really well. They rapidly devolve into bizarre states. If you've never been pelted with shit by a human being or had a fermented piss bomb thrown at you, you really haven't experienced what it's like to work in a maximum-security prison psych ward.

I also worked at McLean Hospital in Boston, in the psychotic disorders unit. They happen to have one of the world's largest collections of human brains, and it was fascinating to examine, for instance, the brain of a schizophrenic and see how different it looked from a normal brain. Clearly, this was not something the guy could have simply snapped out of; the brain was visibly atrophied.

Within this third category of those who are mentally ill are the most dangerous of all people—the rare, functional, and organized psychotic: the Mark David Chapmans and John Hinckleys of the world. Most people who suffer from schizophrenia or psychosis can't leave their houses, let alone organize their thoughts sufficiently to take a shot at the president, but those who can are some dangerous people.

About a year into the graduate program, I figured out I didn't want to sit down in a chair all day long and empathize with people's internal psychological torments and struggles. God bless the people who do, but that's just not for me. I left graduate school, and I left my job at the prison; I knew I wanted to go into the private-security business.

I started out in the security industry in the "systems" side of business, working for a great, small, family-owned business, Alarmex. I was focused on the ghettos of Boston for about a year and a half— Roxbury, Jamaica Plain, and Dorchester—places where you did not need to convince them they had a security problem. Security, or the lack thereof, was a daily issue for the businesses and residents in these gang-infested areas. Subsequently, I worked in a high-end security branch of the big corporate Wells Fargo. If you owned a diamond vault or a bank or if you were a military provider and you had what's called a SCIF (Sensitive Compartmented Information Facility) room where classified documents were handled, Wells Fargo would take care of the security. I covered the diamond vaults in Downtown Boston and the Washington district, and I learned a lot about physical-security assessment, armed robbery, extortions, blackmail, kidnapping—that kind of stuff. I learned about large-scale electronic surveillance during a stint with another big security company but left to start my own firm. Why? Because my experience with the big companies convinced me that they just didn't care about the clients the way I did—or the way the small family-owned Alarmex did. I found that morally offensive, and honestly, it reminded me of criminal thinking—"We want the money but really don't want to do the work." When you've reached agreement with a client and you promise them you're going to do something, it's a sacred agreement. Forget about the contracts; you have to care about it!

My company, Engineered Protection Systems, or EPS, became one of the largest and most successful security firms in Houston, with a client roster that included Six Flags, Goldman Sachs, Exxon, Dow Chemical, and many more. I sold the business in 2000 and went back into corporate, which was a horrible experience. I learned something important about myself, though; I discovered that I am basically unemployable. I think that's true of entrepreneurs in general. Entrepreneurship is often an adaption skill for the unemployable. They have a high likelihood of attention deficit disorder. Maybe they have some issues with authority, but they're innovative and creative in what they do, so they become entrepreneurs.

That was certainly true with me; I worked for this company for a year, and it was like doing time. The only good thing that came out of it was a decade-plus friendship with one of the nation's best security operators, Ray Gilley. But I wasn't built to work for someone else for very long, so about halfway into it, I started another company—this one involved with the integration of physical and digital security. There were a lot more devices appearing that "lived on the network"—network cameras, network surveillance, network-based access control, network intrusion—and I'd started to see the blend of what were once unrelated areas of cybersecurity, IT security and physical security. That company grew fast; I was approached by a venture fund to do a roll-up merger, and we went out and acquired security businesses across Texas and Oklahoma.

At that time, post-9/11, we were focused on something called CFATS, or the Chemical Facility Anti-Terrorism Standards. The Port of Houston and the petrochemical infrastructure by any Homeland Security national-security analysis is a highly likely target for terrorism. If terrorists blew up the refineries here, they'd destroy the economic engine of the US. Because no matter how you feel about it, petrochemical production is critical to our economy. We formed a new company, Infrastruct; there was a small consulting division within it, and this division did unique consulting to law enforcement on computer forensics and training.

We used to run a training course on the establishment of human intel networks in ethnically difficult-to-penetrate communities. We had a couple of Israelis who worked for us, both formerly with Israel's internal security service—known as Shin Bet. The Israelis are very successful at stopping terrorists because they view terrorism as organized crime, and they approach it in the way that we in America approach the Mafia. There are sources of funds, there are people who supply the materials to the suicide bombers, and there are people who transport the suicide bombers. There are people who send money to the families after the suicide bombers detonate; there are guys who get the suicide bombers high. Israelis look at dismantling it as the organized criminal effort that it is, so we started consulting and teaching those ideas to local law enforcement.

By the early 2000s, I decided that I was going to get more into the investigative piece. I met with a number of experts in the fields of surveillance, backgrounds, digital forensics, and litigation support. What became clear to me was that the field was very segmented, with traditional surveillance and background people on one side and computer forensics people on the other. And even within the two groups, segmentation silos existed, which could interfere with seeing the world from the client's perspective. The client likely had a complex issue, which touched various areas of *all* of the above: a problem that did not stay completely in the physical or the digital realm. Yet the industry had few who could address the issues across the various disciplines. I saw a real opportunity and invested in what I knew was going to be a meaningful practice. I also knew that it would allow me to work on a critical skill—rapid and deep problem solving; asymmetrical thinking fueled by an ability to rapidly profile and understand complex systems and competing needs.

I also believe in staying on the right side of what is legal. It is a line that I never cross and frankly don't need to in order to accomplish my work. As an individual and as a firm, we have the skills and the knowledge to resolve things properly.

It was clear from the start that we would need to invest significant money and time into our digital forensic lab. Whether you're an investigator, a private investigator, a law enforcement person, or a combination thereof, if you do not have the skills to follow things from a digital format as well as via traditional means, you're not getting the full picture. You have to be able to go from the computer and mobile forensics networks to traditional investigative surveillance, backgrounds, points of information, connections, interviews: all of it.

That's our edge—combining traditional skills as licensed private investigators with the digital certified computer forensics. In every case I'm going to talk about here, that edge made all the difference to the outcome for our clients because the fact is that most private investigators and local law enforcement just don't have the capacity for digital investigations, and the federal agencies are too busy dealing with drug cartels and terrorists to bother with such problems.

The Internet and digital data have changed everything, from how we track down the bad guys to how we deal with them when we find them. It's changed how criminals find and work their victims, how your spouse cheats on you, how your employee embezzles from you, and how safe your kid is—or isn't.

Each of the cases I'll be talking about is very different, but my point of view is that they all have something to teach us—something valuable regardless of how repulsive the perpetrator is. The fact is I view the criminal enterprise with respect. *If I don't respect it, I can't treat it seriously, and I can't develop a competing system to address it.* It is like respecting the other side in a war. If you don't view the enemy as a real threat, you will get killed.

I start by looking at the individual I'm dealing with: the background, the profile, what the business model is behind his or her actions, and how we can disrupt the economic model behind the behavior, because as I've said, we don't beat people up. Criminals and deviants by and large would prefer a beating to what we do. Most of the people we're dealing with are in that first category of career criminals, and in effect what we say is, "Listen. We know everything about you; we know what you've done. If you don't stop doing what you're doing, we're going to disrupt your ability to run your business or act on your deviant drives." The disruption of the criminal or deviant business or pattern is more feared than anything physical—it disrupts the target's energy cycle from sourcing to processing to harvesting the energy of the ill-gotten gain.

CHAPTER TWO

THE JEWISH UNICORN

One thing I've learned in the course of my investigations is the fact that "smart" is not the same thing as "savvy." So often, I encounter clients who are self-made and wealthy, people who'd score in the genius category on an IQ test. But their emotional intelligence, a.k.a. their EQ, mid- to below-average. Their ability to understand the nuances of emotional chemistry is poor. Is it that they spent all that time amassing their fortunes and forgot to have real relationships? Are they just missing a chip? It's hard to say, but it never ceases to amaze me how many highly intelligent people can be led like lambs to slaughter by predatory criminals. Take what happened to my client in this case.

A brilliant, high-end commodities trader and serial entrepreneur, he had amassed a fairly substantial fortune even by Houston standards, but this client—let's call him Stuart—was referred to us by a law firm because he'd bought himself a problem neither he nor they could handle.

He'd found a *Jewish unicorn.*

While his business endeavors had done well, his personal life was a slow motion car wreck: a series of unhappy endings and dysfunctional relationships with the opposite sex.

He knew that he probably was a bit of a dolt when it came to dealing with women and relationships. A complicating factor was that Stuart was Jewish, which meant his self-selected pool of available women was even more limited. In every major city, there's a Jewish community; Houston's the same way, although ours is more assimilated than most. You wouldn't really notice a Jewish cultural presence here. There are no big delis in the middle of the neighborhood. There are no big signs on kosher butcher shops or bakeries. You could spot the occasional temple, but for the most part, Jews are just part of the larger culture—except when it comes to marriage. There's substantial pressure on Jews from their families and religious leaders not to marry outside the faith, and this guy had been raised to believe that marrying a *shiksa*—disparaging Yiddish terminology for a non-Jewish woman—was tantamount to re-enacting the Holocaust. What people with this kind of problem will often do is basically attempt to buy a relationship. So he went to a specifically Jewish online dating service, looking for love. That's where he first spotted his unicorn.

What is a Jewish unicorn? It is the blond, blue-eyed vision of every Jewish guy's adolescent fantasies. It is the Farah Fawcett poster every man over 50 lusted over in his youth—the Scarlett Johansson/Charlize Theron/Malibu Barbie that your Jewish grandmother told you you'd never have. Like the mermaid, she's a frustrating mix of irresistible allure and impossible fulfillment, and also like the mermaid, she's a mythical creature. But, again, as smart as Stuart was about business, he was hopeless when it came to relationships—especially with the opposite sex.

The Internet has opened all kinds of doors and possibilities, especially for predators. On this same Jewish dating service lurked a beautiful young woman who was looking for exactly the kind of man Stuart was—rich and lonely. She'd had a lot of experience with that kind of man, working as a high-end prostitute since immigrating to the United States a few years before from the former Soviet Bloc. She would do in-calls, where clients would meet her at an apartment kept specifically for this kind of transaction, as well as out-calls, where she'd go to the client. She worked multiple angles, which has become common for sex workers. A lot of them don't have a formal pimp; the guy in the Lincoln, parked around the corner smoking cigarettes while the hooker turns a trick, is a last-millennium cliché, largely replaced with agencies or independent contractors.

In this modern age of cyberprostitution, women will work under various profiles, and this one had multiple websites. She would work one site as the girl next door and sell a girlfriend experience; the client could lie on her bosom and tell her about his long day at work and then have sex with her. She also worked another website where she offered a harder edge: a beautiful model who liked to fuck hard. Some clients she worked through an agency and some she sourced directly.

At the time, this woman was in her early thirties. She'd come to Houston to marry a rich guy and figured the Jewish dating service was a good place to look. She didn't look remotely Jewish; blond, blue-eyed, Nordic, and fit, she looked like a warrior princess in a Conan movie; as my grandma would say, "*Shiksa*, pure." Her cover story was that her family's religious expression had been suppressed by state-imposed atheism, and she was trying now to reconnect with her Jewish heritage. It's a way she could get around knowing nothing about Judaism because she'd grown up in this atheist culture. She started getting involved in the Jewish Community Center and at the temples and preschool, embedding herself in there to wait for the right, rich Jewish guy to come along: one that had what we refer to as a case of *Shiksa* madness—someone searching for a Jewish unicorn.

That dating site is where she first made contact with my client, and she was even better in person than online. Not only was she gorgeous, but she worked at a Jewish daycare center and came across as charming and educated. People have a very degraded view of high-end sex workers; when they hear the word "prostitute," they think of some slinky whore walking down the street with her torn fishnets and a big purse. That's not the case anymore, and it never was fully the case; prostitution has always had a high-end component, never more so than today. From an economic perspective, the supply side has never been more abundant. The demand has never been more abundant, either. This woman had the equivalent of a master's degree—excellent knowledge of wine and food and appreciation for classical music, the arts, and culture. We're talking about someone you could sit and have a stimulating conversation with. She looked classy, not cheap: beautiful hair, skin, and clothes. What do you think a high-end prostitute like that goes for in a major metropolitan market? Try $1,500 to $3,000 for an hour and a half or two.

With my client, however, she had a longer game in view—what we call a long con. Think about it; in a very short period of time, someone with limited language skills comes to a city she's never been in before. Within months, she understands the internal economic model of a community and where the sweet spot is to find her victim.

Only the Internet could have allowed her to figure all that out so quickly. From the time she arrived on the shores to the time she nailed my client, it was about twelve months. She'd been able to transact with customers to make money and to embed herself within this little ethnic enclave, seeding the way for the victim. Now our client comes along, who's, again, a brilliant guy but a pushover for this woman. She knew exactly what he wanted and gave it to him.

Within ninety days of their first date, she was pregnant—thanks to black market fertility drugs. Most men will have intercourse without protection, if the woman is willing—and boy, was she willing! In 120 days, they were married—because our client was so smitten that he could ignore those little fissures, those early warning signs that could have shown her up as a fraud, if only he'd been looking for them.

Of course, about four or five months into it, the fissures become full-blown fault lines. He began to see who this person really was—a hardened former Soviet Bloc operator whose hustle started and ended with her vagina. There was a reason that she'd left the former Soviet Republics, and it wasn't because she wanted to practice her religion freely. But now, as a mother, she felt safe enough to reveal her personality more and more, and guess what? She no longer wanted to fuck our client. She never did. It was a means to an end, and now she'd gained access to his money. She began embezzling money a little at a time and socking it away. She had a game plan.

But she wasn't really a sophisticated, white-collar criminal; she was a blue-collar hustler, a criminal hack, and it also turned out that she was a bit of an idiot. Had she been smarter, she could have gone after him in more sophisticated ways. Instead, she'd buy expensive things and then return them and keep the money. He bought her jewelry, and she'd replace it with cubic zirconia. She was taking little bits of money off the side—$3,000 here, $6,000 there. Finally, about nine months after the kid was born, she filed for divorce.

What she hadn't realized was that in the state of Texas when you're married for such a short period of time, the divorce settlement nets out only to be the gain that occurred while married. They'd only been married, in total, less than a year, and the guy was an entrepreneur. During the period of time that they were married, the total cash and appreciation of these assets that he owned before they were married was not that significant. The state of Texas also has a limit to how much a person has to pay in child support, so it didn't matter that this guy was worth fifty to sixty million dollars. So even though she'd hired herself a big, fancy attorney, she came out of it with about fifty thousand dollars plus the state-defined minimum child support and feeling seriously burned. Certainly, she formed a grudge against her ex that she intended to pay off down the line.

She decided to try her hand at this again. She got a non-disclosure, non-disparaging statement as part of the settlement, so she went back to the well to find another Jewish guy with the same exact MO—same play, different temple. Now her kid was in the Jewish Day Program, so she looked to the potential target to be a semi-distraught single mom with a kid. The next sucker came along, saw this vision of a *shiksa* goddess, and fell for it. The beautiful Jewish unicorn on the hill worked her magic again …

Bingo. In maybe 120 days, she was pregnant with kid number two. But—again!—she didn't do her due diligence on this guy, either. Although his family was wealthy and high profile, they considered him to be a bit of a bumbler—a *schmendrick*—so he didn't have access to any of the family money. She discovered pretty quickly that there really wasn't a pot of gold with this guy either, and she divorced him in a year.

Now she had two kids and two divorces under her belt, and the Houston Jewish community isn't that big, So now she'd become a known quantity, and she realized there wouldn't be a victim number three locally. To augment her income, she went back to turning tricks. A lot of her clients paid her with their credit cards; she'd set up a phony catering service to process the payments, and she did deliver hot dishes, so to speak, but what she then started doing was *recharging*. You'd pay her $1,500 for the trick, and then next week, she'd bang your credit card for another $2,000–$3,000. So what are you going to do about it—complain to your wife? Call the credit card company or the cops? Not likely.

She was also working through an agency and cheating them, too. In the world of prostitution, "agency" is a synonym for "mob front," so she pissed off some fairly significant connected people here in Houston, and they were going to kill her. So she grabbed her kids, who are by now two and four, and she blew town, taking her aunt with her, who she'd hired to be a "nanny."

Our client was supposed to go pick his kid up on a Friday at the apartment for his regular visit. But when he got there, she'd gone. There was fresh milk in the fridge, fresh fruit on the counter; she'd grabbed her iPad and a phone but left two big desktop Macs and one of her phones behind. Nobody home. Her passport was gone, and so were the kids.

He tried to call her—no answer. He had no idea what had happened. He secured the apartment and called the police. He got a police report that says "missing persons" for her and the kids and the aunt. And he waited.

A week later, he received an email from her that said, "Sorry I didn't tell you, but I had to leave the country with the kids. Grandpa so-and-so died. We're at the funeral. We're going to visit family, and we'll be back within a couple of weeks. I'm sorry it seemed so rushed, but everything's okay." He's not 100 percent sure about that, but what's he going to do at this point in time?

Two weeks went by. She emailed him a couple other times, sent him some pictures of the kids, one of them taken in Paris. Sent him another picture of the kids outside Paris, in the Dijon region: "Here are the kids. They're having a good time. Not a big deal." Then she wrote that she was coming back and to come get them at the airport. He went to the airport to meet the flight they were coming back on. But there was no such flight, and the emails stop. That was when he realized that he had a serious problem on his hands. That's when he called his lawyer, and his lawyer called us.

Europe is a very large continent, especially if you do not want to be found. Each one of these countries has its own law enforcement. The Swiss and the Italians may or may not talk with each other. The French and English may or may not talk with each other. What's considered illegal in France may not be considered illegal in England. You have an international law enforcement agency, Interpol, that's really nothing more than a cooperative intelligence network. But at that point in time, was this actually a law enforcement issue? What law had she broken? She went to Europe. He knew she went to Europe. She said she went to Europe. Maybe she was out backpacking in the Black Forest. But his instincts were telling him it was something more.

And this time, his instincts were right: Now she had something that these two guys both cared about—their kids—and she was going to use that as leverage to settle the scores.

Both men called the FBI. They called local law enforcement. Local law enforcement spoke to the FBI, but what were the local police going to do about someone who abducted the kids? She hadn't killed your kids. They were not showing up in child pornography movies. The kids had gone to Europe with their biological mother. Where was that going to prioritize on a major metropolitan police department's risk levels? About zero, even for a well-to-do person who's well connected. The Houston Police Department didn't have an office outside Paris in the Dijon region. The FBI was worried about terrorism; they simply could not be that concerned about what appeared to be custodial abduction.

We had our first meeting with the client and started drilling down to what he knew about his ex: "Who is this woman? What is her background? How did she make a living before she met you?" One of the things he didn't know about her (which we discovered later, when we went through the computers) was how she'd made a living before they'd met. He never knew that she was a high-end prostitute. That happens all the time; people just don't see what's right in front of them.

When I looked at her initially, the profiler in me said, "She doesn't look like a Russian woman of Jewish descent." She looked like she was Finnish or Swedish. Hell, she could have been from Iceland. We couldn't find any records on her. There were no utilities in her name. She had prepaid cell phones. She had no credit history. What that told me was this was someone who was making a living on the black market economy. Clearly, someone who looked like her from the former Soviet Republics, who'd been here for six months, lived this way by selling herself, period. She wasn't living her kind of lifestyle by working as a nanny. She was probably turning two or three tricks a day, which amounted to a lot of cash.

We also profiled our client: Why would this guy have gotten involved with her? He was a very interesting guy and very forthcoming, and as we talked, it became pretty apparent that he had never been able to establish any sort of real relationships with women. He'd never had any multiyear relationships with someone on his level; his view of relationships was pretty transactional. That helped us to understand the perpetrator/victim dynamic here.

When we went to examine her abandoned apartment, we spotted the two large Mac desktop computers, which again was kind of unusual. Why would someone like that have two giant computers sitting in her apartment? We had our forensic tech image the computers, creating an exact copy of those computer drives, as they existed on the computer at that moment in time. We took the forensic copy to our lab and processed the drive, running recovery software that allowed us to access even files she'd deleted. She'd had these computers for about three years, and there was a trove of information. We recovered literally tens of thousands of emails.

We were able to recover text communications and her browser history—including all the websites that she was using to solicit herself as a prostitute, including her username and passwords to the sites. That became important, because she'd left the United States with basically nothing, which meant she was going to have to get back to work selling sex in Europe.

A lot of the emails were in Russian, so we had to bring in a translator, and we were able to dig up her whole plan of finding a rich

Jewish guy. We also discovered how furious she was that she hadn't gotten half of our client's assets at the divorce, as she'd imagined she would, instead of $1,700 a month in child support, which she made in a single afternoon from one trick. As we went through this stuff, we could see that she was gone and wasn't planning on coming back. Unfortunately, we'd gotten these computers about three and a half weeks after she'd left, so we'd missed opportunities to catch up with her. And she'd changed her passwords, so we could no longer track her movements.

But everything that goes on the Internet has an Internet protocol (IP) address attached to it. From the IP addresses, we were able to identify an area where she had been, which was a little distance from Paris. The client realized by then that the Houston Police Department wasn't going to do anything for him, so he authorized us to go. He flew us to Europe; we started tracking her from that last email that she'd sent.

We chased her across Europe for almost four months. She was very sophisticated at hiding herself. She eventually started not only changing the passwords but also her username and profile on a lot of different websites. One of my guys who was there with me is a good investigator, a former Marine Corps scout. He had a couple of tours in Iraq as part of the US team tracking down war criminals in all these shithole villages all over Iraq. One of the other guys with us happened to speak French and Italian. We knew she wouldn't go back to Russia: too much competition at low prices. So a high-end prostitute wouldn't trick in Russia. She'd trick in Paris or London or Monaco or Berlin or The Hague.

We knew from the computer forensics that she had historically transacted in Paris, and we were sure that's where she would be based.

We knew she liked to transact out of higher-end hotels; we also knew she was dragging two kids around with her the whole time, so if she had an apartment, it would have been for her and the kids and the aunt and would not be where she was tricking.

We dug into traditional detective work. We went to all the high-end hotels around Paris. We flashed her picture, and we gave a little money to the doorman, so if he saw her he'd give us a call. We paid visits to a lot of the Jewish day schools around Paris on the hope that maybe she had now gone to look for a French Jewish guy to whom she could do what she'd done in the United States—and that's where we got our first lead. One of the schools told us she'd come in to find out about registering the kids there, and she'd given them an address where she was staying. It was a time-share flat; she'd taken it for a month and paid cash but was gone before we arrived.

We were now about three months into it. We'd heard absolutely nothing from her, and the client hadn't received an email, a telephone call, nothing. None of the hotels or people had seen her, which may or may not have been true. She may have paid them not to say anything.

Finally, the other shoe dropped; she sent an email to our client, laying out her terms: "I know you can't find me, and if I want, I can make sure you never see your kid again. I'll take both my kids to an orphanage in Dagestan where no one will ever find them. If you want to see your kid again, you're going to have to pay me five million dollars. No negotiation. You have five days."

We knew she could do it; they could literally just disappear. We also feared they could be sold into child prostitution. When we analyzed the risk for the client we said, "Here's the deal; she doesn't care. These guys are going to sell these kids off to white slavery."

These were two beautiful kids, gorgeous children; I suspected that was her plan, especially since we discovered that she had grown up in child prostitution herself. This woman came from a very dark place, and what she was willing to do to make a living and survive was beyond what we'd imagine in the West.

But she'd made a mistake because, again, the IP address was discoverable in the email. Oftentimes, IP addresses are not static. They change; one day it may be 1.2.3.4.8.9. The next day it could be a completely different number, giving only a general idea of the location: "It's in Southern California," but nothing more specific than that. But on this particular day, she sent an email from somewhere that had a static IP address: an apartment complex in a rundown area near Paris. There was a hostel right across the street from it, where we set up a surveillance post. Four or five days later, we saw the aunt come into the building: not the target nor the kids but the aunt.

We watch the aunt for about a week and a half; the woman and the kids were nowhere to be seen. Finally, the aunt got in her car and drove off for five or six hours to a small town in the Dijon region. Because we had two vehicles, we could follow her at a very discreet distance, and she was totally oblivious to the fact she had a tail. She pulled up to a house, out of which came the target and the two kids.

I called my client and told him to gas up his Gulfstream and come to the nearest airport; we'd pick him up there. We wanted him in the van when we went after the kids, because they needed to see someone that they knew. He flew in that night.

That morning, she took the little kids out to the park, and we pulled up in the van. When she saw us grab her son, she went wild, scratching and screaming. We got both kids, pushed them into the van and took off for the airport where the Gulfstream was waiting.

Within half an hour we were airborne, on our way back to the States. When we'd grabbed the kids, the little boy was holding a diaper bag. A cell phone was in it. When we got back, we forensically imaged that phone and were able to find out that not only was she transacting as a prostitute but that she had, in fact, found a new Jewish guy to scam in the exact same way. We believe that's where matters stand today.

Now our client has more of a sense of security concerning his kid. The two fathers had done the proper court work before we picked the children up in Paris; the fathers were named the primary custodians, and the prostitute had her rights stripped from her, so there were no issues with US immigration. Obviously, she never showed up in court for any of the hearings, so she lost all of her rights.

As is our standard practice, we asked ourselves what we'd learned from the case and what could we do better next time. A few thoughts rise to the top. First, there is no such thing as a Jewish unicorn. Jews don't come from far off Nordic countries—only Santa Claus does. However, the Jewish male desire to find his Jewish unicorn will remain a cultural wrinkle. The search continues.

Secondly, had the client contacted us sooner, a lot of what he had to go through could have been avoided. If something looks bad, it probably *is* bad, and if you have access to that digital information, then you can find out. If someone's doing something wrong today, there's going to be a digital signature to it, and there was a huge digital signature to this case. It was all because of those computers in the apartment. This case eventually wound up well, but it cost our client a lot to keep a crew traveling across Europe for three months.

But if he'd paid her—and for a moment there he was considering it—would she have taken another bite at it? Probably. Would she have dumped these kids off in the middle of nowhere and then tried to bleed the guy more? I'm guessing she would. If you will pay once, you will pay twice. The adversary in these types of situations has the advantage of pre-planning. The victim's thought process is clouded with stress and dread.

We're not law enforcement. What we did was to help our client solve this problem and get his kid back. As much as the perpetrator deserved to face justice, that's not what we were paid to do. When you're doing private resolution issues like this, it's important that the person have an out. When you don't want to give someone that out, then it becomes a law enforcement issue. As horrible as that sounds, she's probably victimizing someone else right now. We just said, "You've had enough fun with us. We're taking the kids and going home."

Ultimately, we found out that our prostitute was also on the lam from her city in Dagestan, where she and her aunt had been involved in all kinds of bad stuff like embezzlement cases, elder abuse, and elder theft. The aunt was also a multi-career criminal with a record across Europe.

Fortunately for my client, we were able to keep his son out of Mom's family business.

CHAPTER THREE

COACH CREEPER

The relationship between a coach and a talented young athlete is very special and very close. Nobody has more authority in a driven young athlete's life, not even his or her parents. The student athlete's attitude can border on worship. Sometimes it can get a little too close.

That was the case with a gymnastic coach that a client of ours encountered via his young, driven daughter.

The thing that's important to understand about these cases is when there's a violation of the coach-student relationship with a sexual element to it, there always has to be a microcosm in which that person operates. Typically in this kind of case, people use the word "pedophile" to describe the perpetrator. But actually in the literature of the clinical or law enforcement world, a pedophile means something very different, very specific, and rarer. In this case and many like it, they are opportunistic sex offenders who have similar characteristics to pedophiles, but they're different in numerous material ways.

In the cases I've dealt with in the competitive amateur sports world, the offenders resemble pedophiles in that they center on a particular desired object or obsession—and there's a pattern to it, whether it involves twelve-year-old prepubescent boys or sixteen-year-old blonde women. I have found that these offenders are extremely patient. I think parents who haven't been exposed to people like this misunderstand the degree of discipline that they have. As a normal human being, you think having sex with an underage boy or a prepubescent girl is hugely offensive; the mere thought is clouded with so much repulsion, taboo, revulsion, and injustice that it's hard to even talk about it. When you do talk about it with someone, you can see the body language change, and the conversation becomes very uncomfortable. Whenever you hear about these cases, the first thing anyone says is always, "How the hell could that guy, who I've known for years/played golf with/worked with, be a pedophile?"

In this case, the guy in question entered the field as a gym coach, where he developed enough of a reputation that if you were a family in the community with a daughter who was good enough to vie for an Ivy League gymnastics scholarship, he was the guy who could give her the necessary competitive edge. When a coach also happens to be a sexual predator, as this one was, he is a master at manipulating not only the individual but also her family and the setting as a whole. They are masters of this microsystem because they're operating a real business, they're doing real coaching, and they're looking for their next victim.

In this case, that's exactly what happened. This family's daughter had been doing gymnastics since she was a little girl and was good enough that a college scholarship seemed like a reasonable hope. When her parents first encountered this guy—let's call him Bob— she was a freshman in high school. The family had seen Bob at national events and was impressed by his star power and the buzz he generated. He wouldn't work with just *anyone*: only the best of the best. It was like a very exclusive cult, and these parents were eager to get their daughter, let's call her Heather, into his capable hands. This is normal for a high-powered coach; it's also normal for someone who's an opportunistic sex offender—a real groomer, patient but ready to strike when it all lines up.

The family met Bob, and he said to the girl, "I've watched you at these tournaments for the last few years. I only pick a few students every year to work with, and I think that can be you, but you're going to need to train like I want you to train. You're going to have to do everything I tell you to do." Heather and her parents were thrilled; he was charging them about three times what the average student is charged, but based on the family's goals and what they thought he could do for them, from their point of view it was not a material expense.

Heather, who was fourteen at the time, started training with him. For the first year, there was really nothing unusual. She went to training, and since she was not driving yet, Mom took her. The coaching was going well. There was a lot of one-on-one time but nothing particularly atypical. In retrospect, what you see is he really got very close to the girl, learning a lot about her particular psychological issues, her family dynamics, and so forth. He also got extremely close to her mother.

One thing these cases have in common when it's a male coach/female victim scenario is that typically the father is either not present or his attention is on making the means for the family. The guy was actually an extremely good dad and involved, but Mom ran the home. That's important because this is exactly the profile that the perpetrator was looking for. To be his potential victim, the girl had to be over sixteen years old, brunette, with an athletic build, and very all-American looks, with a father who was out of town a lot or gone altogether. Plus the family had to have money. We ended up concluding that this was part of his thrill, getting the family to finance the deflowering of their precious daughter. It was part of his kick. It wasn't just sex; it was winning, even above the dad. There was almost something like a class and cultural dominance component to it.

The coach in this case was Eastern European, former Soviet Bloc, from a Russian Orthodox background, and was in his late 40s. He was no Tom Cruise; if you looked at his face, you'd swear he had served time in some Soviet gulag. He looked like his face had been caved in with a shovel, like a fifth-rate boxer. This wasn't a guy that a young woman might easily fall for. But he was patient; he knew that if he started her out as his pupil at fourteen, he'd have her where he wanted her at sixteen. When she was fifteen and driving on her own, he started meeting her for psychological strategy sessions at Starbucks. (Side note: What's funny here is that most people see coffee shops as a place to get your lattés or Americanos or your tall coffees, but I'll bet you 20 percent of the cases I've seen that involve extramarital affairs or some sort of inappropriate meet-up occur at a coffee shop. If you're doing something wrong and you're under seventy, there's a good chance it includes rendezvous at a coffee shop.)

He met her at Starbucks four or five times. On the fifth or sixth time, he walked her to the car to be gentleman-like. By the twentieth meeting, he asked if he could hold her hand on the way to the car. By the thirtieth meeting, and now we're getting close to the time she'll be sixteen, he asked for a kiss. He began to counsel her to cut herself loose from her friends, her family, and especially her father, because these relationships were "interfering" with her training. Meanwhile he was pumping up her ego, telling her she had the gifts to go the Olympics if she'd just do as he told her, which just wasn't true, but how could she resist? He was a Svengali, and she was utterly taken in. He manipulated her in ways like this: "Look, if you only paid more attention in our psychological coaching sessions, if you allowed me to love you as much as I want to love you and believe in you, then this would be possible. If you would put aside these stereotypes and these artificial barriers that you create because of our age difference and our cultural difference, maybe you could accomplish your goal. Is this all you're about? Does your definition of being a young, rich American princess mean that the only person you can be in love with is a nineteen-year old rich boy who's going to Duke? What if truly loving someone, regardless of his age and ethnic background, transformed your life and allowed you to become what you were truly meant to be? Are you a big enough person to do that, or are you so small-minded, like every other American, that you will limit yourself?"

That was the dialogue, and it was very powerful. When on top of that, oblivious parents say things like, "Why are you not committed to the coaching by the coach? He says you're not working hard enough," any young woman might feel herself triangulated. Add to that, he started to text her as part of this ongoing grooming process, preparing her psychologically for the statutory rape he'd been planning. At that point, he began leaving a digital trail, which turned out to be critically important.

In this day and age, opportunistic sex offenders like Bob groom their victims via emails and texts. Such evidence is going to be powerful, because it eliminates the deniability that could get offenders off the hook in the past. Before this, often the victim wouldn't speak up about what was going on until well after the fact, when the DNA evidence is gone, and she finally says, "Mom, I can't handle it anymore. I slept with the coach."

Mom calls the cops: "Was she raped?"

"Well, yeah, but statutorily."

"Is there DNA evidence?"

"No, we washed her clothes."

"Did she tell anybody else about it?"

"No."

So the cops go over to see Coach. "Coach, Annie says that you had sex with her."

"What is she talking about? I never had sex with her; she's infatuated with me. Anyone will tell you she's got puppy eyes for me. I never had sex with her. I'm cutting her out of my club. I can't deal with these kinds of allegations. By the way, she's a dirty little slut. I know everything about her. She gave Billy a blowjob at the school dance. And I bet she didn't tell her parents that she smoked marijuana and that she owns a sex toy."

So the detective comes back and says, "Is this true?"

"Well, yeah."

The opportunistic sex offender who's also intelligent—as in the above hypothetical case—is an accomplished test master. When a cops shows up at the door and asks him these questions, he's already rehearsed the scene in his mind a thousand times, with every scenario you can imagine: "We have the soiled panties, we have a photograph, a witness said so-and-so." He's got a bullshit answer memorized for every possible thing they might throw at him. His victim doesn't have answers, and her family doesn't either, *because the family is absorbing a crisis, and he's mastering that crisis.* This is a sophisticated person who's oftentimes running a significant operation. He's not a psychopath. He knows the difference between right and wrong; he just struggles to control himself. Ultimately, the person is not controlled by his mental illness. He does have the ability to control himself, not like people who can't leave their house because they have to wash their hands 400 times a day—although he too has a compulsion. It's a much scarier version, in some ways, because it's muted and amalgamated, if you will, into the social fabric in which he functions. So he's careful not to target the daughter of a high-powered lawyer or the daughter of a private investigator or the daughter of an investigative journalist. He's chosen this girl in part because her family isn't in the habit of dealing with guys like him. Life hasn't taken a big enough shit on them yet for them to be suspicious of everyone who comes in contact with them. They're more gullible, and when their kids finally do tell, they're devastated.

But Heather didn't tell—at least not at first and not out loud. Her grades started to slip, though, and her parents began noticing odd changes in her behavior, changes that revealed her to be under some unknown stress. Heather knew that having a sexual relationship with her forty-something Eastern European dog-faced coach was not how her story was supposed to be written. But she was in it and now started snapping at her parents. This went on for four or five months, until the parents began to see that something was seriously off, at which time they told her that no matter what was happening, she could always talk to them about it.

So she finally told them that at the same time the coach had been training her, he'd also been working her into a relationship, and it had evolved into him texting her at all hours of the night, bullying her, and saying to her that if she was not cooperative, he would ignore her in training the next day. He'd pile it on at high-stress moments, like right before a competition; "You wouldn't kiss me last night, so I'm not going to coach you." Once he got inside her head, he knew the buttons that he could push to get what he wanted from her.

What finally made her report him to her parents? He and she would travel out of state sometimes on competitions, and while a lot of times he would travel with her parents, this particular time she traveled with a group of girls. He texted her from his room to come and help him with some baggage for their performance, and when she walked in, she found him standing there naked. No doubt in his mind this was the moment where he was going to consummate the relationship. But instead, she fled, probably realizing for the first time that this relationship was out of control and that it had gotten to a point where she was going to be exposing herself to some kind of sexual violence.

So she finally told her parents. Of course, they became frantic because she also told them the story about seeing him nude. The parents immediately asked, "Did you have sex with him? Did it go any further?" No, no, and no. Of course, the parents were in a difficult position because this guy had timed his stunt perfectly; the towel drop occurred two weeks before her applications were going to college—which also required a letter from him. So now he'd created a dilemma for the parents and the kid; if they did blow the whistle, were they also destroying her future?

At the first pass, when you ask someone to tell you all of the truth, what I've seen in my business is that no one ever tells the full truth immediately. You have to go back over things with people two or three times. People forget things, and if they're embarrassed by something—if something is taboo or risqué—it's a natural human thing to want to leave it alone.

So the parents freaked out: What were they going to do? She was in the middle of applying to college, and there was another key competition coming up in a week. The daughter said there'd been no sex.

I had done some business work for a friend of Heather's dad. He called his friend the next day, really distraught, and told his friend what happened. His friend said, "I suggest you call my friend Dan. He's an investigator and also does forensic work." So he called me. I set up a visit with the mom and the dad: not the daughter initially, but just her parents, to kind of get a sense of what they knew.

As we were sitting there talking, I asked, "What kind of cell phone does your daughter have?" Normally when you ask that question in a meeting, people want to know why. The reason I want to know is because if there's evidence, it's going to be on that phone. The problem we had in this case was that there would be no DNA evidence. It was going to be "he said, she said." The only evidence we were going to find in this case was whatever was on that phone; that was the key thing we needed to discover.

It's always interesting to me when parents resist the idea of forensically imaging their kids' phones to retrieve the data on them. As Americans, we're not comfortable with eavesdropping, and there's also some element of not wanting to see what's on there. But the fact is you own the phone, she's under eighteen years old, and you have the right to look at everything on that device.

So they covertly got the phone from the daughter when she was asleep. Sitting in the driveway of their home, we forensically imaged a copy of her iPhone. It took us about twenty-four hours to process the data, and we found ten thousand text messages between her and the coach. It actually had maxed out the space on the phone over a period of about a year and a half. Those text messages laid out exactly what had been going on. A lot of it she'd thought had been deleted. About a year into the communications, I think he must have read an article on mobile forensics because he began directing her to use a different app, WhatsApp, which is a Wi-Fi texting app.

A Wi-Fi app doesn't show up on your phone history. It just shows up as data. If I text you and I look at my record, it shows this number to that number. The actual text itself on the WhatsApp application is only on the WhatsApp server, not on the phone, so the ability to recover the texting information from these Wi-Fi apps is much more limited and in some cases impossible. So although we had ten thousand text messages, I assume there were probably three times that number because they switched to this Wi-Fi app.

What's interesting about the communication is how you could really see the progression. From my perspective, it was highly useful. Normally, I don't get to see that degree of history in an ongoing conversation between the victim and the perpetrator to see exactly how the perpetrator grooms the victim over a period of time.

One of the things that we recovered on her phone is what we refer to as the power shot. The power shot is when a guy texts a picture of his erect penis. They always do it the same way; they put the forearm under the erect penis, and it's like, boom, there it is. When we do the forensic recovery, we always ask, do we have a power shot or not? If you can see the guy's face in the power shot, like if he's taken a selfie in the mirror, that's the one we're looking for, and in this case, we *did* get the full power shot—though she hadn't told her parents that in the first pass.

As a practiced predator, I know that a suspected offender can create doubt in almost any one-on-one situation if there's no DNA evidence: "I accidently sent her that photo; she found it on my phone and sent it to herself; she became obsessed with me, and I caught her one time on my phone; yes, I had a picture of myself with my dick hanging over my wrist but that was to my girlfriend. What the hell? I live in a country where I can't send a quality power shot to my loved one? I mean, we have the right to be perverted. It's an American tradition."

I had to break it to her parents. Every father I've ever sat with in this situation always says the same thing: "I want to kill that motherfucker." And I get it.

But I told him, "I don't think you want to do that. Let me tell you why. First of all, you're going to go to jail, and then second of all, you've lived a pretty decent, nice life; you have a nice home and a nice family. Granted, this is a disturbing event that's happening in your life, but do you think you want to have the experience of putting a projectile through someone's chest or head? Do you know what that actually looks like—the amount of blood that comes out, the backsplash when you pop someone in the head? Killing another human being is a fairly graphic thing to do and really not something I advise most people to experience. It doesn't psychologically process well for most folks."

A dad might also say, "Maybe we should just break his knees." Here's the problem with breaking his knees. First of all, I'm not going to do that for you; we're not into "wet work." We don't break peoples' knees. But the fact of it is guys like him are prepared for a beating. In fact, what I've seen is that it can actually be part of their fantasy; they get caught by the girl's dad, and the dad beats them—because in some way that absolves them of their sin. I've heard it from the mouths of sex offenders that they are prepared to take a beating. So from a utilitarian perspective, it's not an effective approach, and you go to jail for aggravated assault—plus the guy might actually beat you up, right? Let's not pretend that the outcome of a physical assault on another human being is always predictable. And again, from a biohazard standpoint, physical assaults tend to be fairly gruesome. Teeth and blood and bodily fluids are all over the place. It's nasty.

I usually suggest that something much worse for the perp would be actually forcing him to face justice in the sport in which he's so exalted, damaging him in his position in the community and effectively ending his ability to go after future victims. There are really two issues in play here: One is seeking justice for your daughter, but the other is preventing this from happening to others.

Let's say the parents consider their options and finally tell me, "Dan, nothing is going to happen to this piece of shit. He's going to deny everything that happened and go back and continue coaching. All we really want is for this guy to stay away from our daughter. We don't want him to call our daughter or see our daughter; that's all we want." Remember, I'm not a cop, I'm not a psychologist; I'm working for the family on what their goals are, and I could accomplish that goal without much trouble. I would recover some of the text messages, I'd get the picture of the guy's power shot, I'd go pay the guy a visit, and I would tell him, "If you ever get near the girl again, everything I just showed you is going right to the police. At this point in time, I'm going to assume that everything I've seen is simply a miscommunication and I don't get it, right? But let's say, for instance, I do get it, I'm going to turn it over to the police, and if I do, it's going to be bad for you. Once I turn it over to them, there's no turning back, because it's out of my hands."

In 98 percent of cases like this guy's, he's going to score that off to a lost opportunity. He's going to mourn the fact that he put a lot of good time and effort into a promising victim. He's going to adjust his methods, and next time he moves to score, he'll do it smarter. That's how he'll think. But in this particular case, the family decided that they wanted both to seek justice and to stop him from having access to future victims.

The question is how to do that. The answer is to go hunting for other victims. How do you potentially find the other victims of a guy who has had a career of coaching hundreds if not thousands of people? The answer is that you have to assume from an evidentiary standpoint that he chose his victim based on certain criteria that are apparent: her look, her age, the situation that she comes from—his ideal profile.

Remember, I know in the background that's how these guys think. It's not as random as it appears, it's as thoughtful as it appears—and the fact it had taken a long time for him to make his move told me what kind of offender that this guy was. He was a thoughtful offender and a planner, a guy who probably had a certain construct that he was operating under.

What's kind of nice about this sport is that very extensive records are kept of all the competitors as well as who their coaches are. Based on that information, we were able to go back in the archives and mine the people who'd been with him over a period of time. We immediately filtered out all the boys and any of the girls that didn't have the look he preferred, and we focused on a list of about seventy-five women who could have met the profile.

We then looked at which percentage of them went on to the National Collegiate Athletic Association (NCAA), because we knew that this was most likely part of how he groomed each victim, by holding the collegiate promise over her as a way to cross over that bridge and get past her resistance. We cut the list down to about thirty. The list was over ten years old, so we went to Facebook, and we found six of those women who resembled our victim. We went about contacting them and were able to track down three women who had experienced the exact same thing. The amazing thing about it was that it stretched back fifteen years, one after the other after the other. There was a crossover point where they all had started being groomed, some as early as thirteen, some as late as fifteen, and he had actually had sex with the other three. He had actually taken the virginity of all three, and one of them told us that he had gotten so aggressive that she considered it not only statutory rape but violent rape. He had held her down. In that particular case, we didn't have text messages or emails, because it had occurred before those kinds of communications became common. In the case of the woman who had been his victim in 2008/2009, there had been texting, but she had changed her cell phone carrier, and text messages are not stored by the telecom provider. The NSA might have a copy, but I don't have access to that. Text messages are stored on the device, so if I don't have the device or you've factory reset the device, it's gone. We were unable to recover that information, so there was no digital evidence.

In those cases, we set the victims up with a formal forensic interview. As soon as I identified who they were and that they had

had a sexual relationship with this coach when they were underage, I stopped the conversation. I said, "Listen, I don't want to ask anymore questions. If you're okay with it, I'm going to get you on the phone with a forensic interviewer". This is a formally trained forensic sex crimes interviewer who is an expert at getting a full story out of a victim. There's a whole structure of how you go about doing a formal forensic interview. As an established firm, we're able to reach out to a large group of specialists. The interviewer conducted formal forensic interviews of these three other victims and a formal forensic interview with our victim.

The gymnastics association is part of a program called SafeSport that's in place to stop things like this from happening to participants. Working as a team with the attorney and our forensic investigator, we put together a report documenting that, based on the digital evidence (i.e., the texting on the phone and the power shot) along with the forensic interviews of our victim and the three other victims, there was a consistent pattern of grooming behavior. The words the suspected offender used, the methods by which he'd engendered the relationships, the points of pressure that he would use; if you lined it all up, everything was the same in each case.

What we discovered from that was a dangerous person: someone who, if given the right ecosystem to operate in, had no limit to how many victims he could collect. His methods became more sophisticated as the cases moved on. We all embrace modern technology, and so do sex offenders. He became more familiar with how to use technology to help manipulate his victims, and he became quite skilled at it.

When we eventually presented this case, the critical thing was that it was no longer "he said, she said"; it was "they said, he did." That made for a much more powerful case than a one-on-one.

This case never went out to the criminal courts; it was addressed as a violation of the SafeSport rules under gymnastics, and they informed Bob that an investigation had begun on his violation. They held a tribunal. In the tribunal, the victim was able to present witnesses, and the other victims testified, too. Of course he denied that any of this had ever happened; he presented about thirty other witnesses that testified that he was a great guy and a great coach. The truth of the matter was that he *was* a decent guy and a great coach unless you were a sixteen-year old brunette girl from a wealthy family. It was clear that he was a very well-regarded person in the sport: he also happened to be a serial sex offender, according to his profile. So to conclude, he was kicked out of the sport, and while he hasn't faced criminal charges, the fact is that without this microcosm in which he operated, it will be much more difficult for him to source victims in the future.

In a perfect world with complete justice, would it have been best if all parties had agreed to pursue criminal charges? The answer is *yes*, but it's a very difficult standard to prove. And again, it gets back to the fact that we're not cops. We work toward what our clients want to accomplish, and in this particular case, we felt we accomplished the goal. The coach was severely restricted in his ability to source and victimize young women like our client. A happy ending? No, not really. Happy endings are for movies and romance novels. In my line of work, it's almost always an unhappy ending—but it's the best of the worst options. The client is satisfied that we have mitigated the downside and, if we are lucky, brought a sense of justice to the issue. Maybe not judicial justice, but justice nonetheless.

CHAPTER FOUR

MY EMPLOYEE...
MY EMBEZZLER

You've heard of death by a thousand cuts? That can happen to a business when a trusted employee is using his or her position of trust to slowly drain it dry, sending payments to fictitious companies or using its funds to cover expenses that are clearly not business related. When it comes to embezzlement, sometimes a small operation can turn out to have a surprisingly long reach—and that was the situation with this case.

It was late on a Friday afternoon when we got the call. Friday is typically a busy time for private investigators, because just before the weekend is the time when people who've been suspecting they might be in some sort of exposure or risk finally decide that they are, indeed, facing a crisis. And that's when they start looking for someone to handle it.

This crisis call came from a CFO who was based outside of Houston in Shreveport, Louisiana. She told me there were indications that the CEO's administrative assistant had been embezzling from the company: Some high-end watches had been shipped to the company; there had been requests for receipts and documents for different things that had been slow in coming back or hadn't come back at all.

But again, it was nothing completely out of the ordinary in a company like this; this was a family office, as we call them, a company basically formed by a wealthy individual with investments in probably seventy different companies and other various holdings: real estate, parking, investments in technology companies, various funds, and bonds. These holdings were managed out of this relatively small office. The accounting staff for this guy's office was very small: just the CFO and a bookkeeper—who was located in an office in another city. But if you looked at all the companies in which the CEO was the majority investor or stockholder, he probably had about a thousand employees. He was someone who on a daily basis moved hundreds of thousands to millions of dollars between companies, banks, and credit facilities and between new ventures and old ventures.

The CFO said they were not sure yet what this administrative assistant was involved in, but it was clear that there was enough of a problem that she was going to end up being terminated. This admin worked in very close proximity to the CEO and founder of the company; in fact, she literally worked inside his office. The CFO told us that she thought the amount stolen was relatively small, compared to their holdings; somewhere between fifteen and thirty thousand dollars.

I told the CFO we would need access to the suspect's computers over the weekend, because before talking with her, we needed to see what she'd been up to. Typically, if someone has been in a position a while (she had been in the position for three years), and if they've been embezzling for a long period of time, they tend to get messy. They're not so cautious about what goes onto their computers.

That always surprises people; we're often asked, "Why would you bother forensically imaging the company's computer? Clearly, somebody who's stealing wouldn't be so stupid as to do it on company computers and on company property." I haven't found that to be true at all. I find that once someone gets into the froth of the crime and it starts generating some money, they really turn into pigs, almost literally. For some reason, people who are embezzling money consume stuff in a shockingly voracious manner.

When you're non-criminal, you'd assume that a person who'd embezzled more than a million dollars over three years would have stashed a pile of that stolen money somewhere, right? But if you have a normal job and you're living a normal life and working, it's kind of hard to spend a ridiculous sum of money like that if you're not acquiring an asset. You could buy a million-dollar house, but if you're just spending money on smaller consumer items, it's actually kind of a difficult thing to do. You've got to spend intensely and consume intensely to burn through it—and that's what I see over and over in cases like this one.

Another of my cases offers a good example. We were investigating an accountant who was embezzling from his client. The client had suspicions and hired us. We did some criminal and background searches on the person; nothing criminal popped up, but we saw a history of civil disputes between him and some of his clients where there were allegations of financial misappropriations.

I decided to meet with the accountant myself under the pretense that his boss was looking at investing in my security firm. We agreed to meet for breakfast at a place in Houston called Buffalo Grille (famous for their plate-size fruit pancakes!), and he told me that his wife, who also worked for my client, would be joining us. I was about two minutes late for the meeting, and by the time I got there, he and his wife had already started eating, which I thought was a little unusual. It wasn't like I was fifteen minutes late. Weirder yet, there was barely room at the table for me to sit down and to join them. There were stacks of pancakes, there were biscuits, there was bacon, there was sausage, there was fruit; it was like I had stumbled into a lumberjack's buffet. I'm not a small guy, and I have a decent appetite, but I have rarely seen anyone consume food with the gusto and greed I witnessed that morning. The guy was eating pancakes with a fork in one hand and dipping a biscuit in butter with the other, alternating bites, and then he'd snatch a slice of bacon or a sausage and eat it in a gulp. Syrup was being sloshed around.

It was grotesque; I couldn't eat. I ended up ordering oatmeal and taking about two bites of it. His wife was doing the same thing, and they were talking while they were eating. He was a huge guy, 400 pounds at a guess, and his face was slick with sweat. It was like being in the presence of a human swine, and I knew at once that, *yep, this guy is an embezzler.*

I've noticed over twenty years that this is a vibe that's critical for me to pick up in embezzlement cases. I know when I have a real embezzlement case, because a human swine tends to be involved. Once embezzlers have figured out how to get the money out, it becomes a pig fest like you cannot believe, and it makes no logical sense! That's why the first thing I look for on a suspect's computer and web history is online ordering. Usually I find a lot of frenzied activity—and that's just the tip of the iceberg—the behavioral manifestation of what's probably a much bigger case.

Returning now to the original case, please remember, the CFO told us in the initial call that we were talking about an embezzlement of maybe fifteen to thirty thousand dollars ...

We went in first thing Saturday morning, and we forensically imaged the suspected embezzler's laptop computer. We discovered she had two other phones on the company tab that the client didn't know about. These were hidden in her desk: always a very bad sign. We also forensically imaged those phones. In the process of documenting everything in her office, we came across a basket full of receipts underneath her desk—not a little basket either but one the size of a small laundry basket. It was filled with credit card statements, receipts, and bills totaling hundreds of thousands of dollars. This was a woman who was being paid $90,000 a year, but looking at the receipts I could see that she was spending tens of thousands every month.

As we sifted through the digital evidence, we found out she'd been ordering stuff online, crazy amounts of it: ten Keurig coffee pots at a time and hundreds of the coffee pods to go with them. She was ordering fifteen or twenty pillows, fifteen to twenty airline gift cards in $500 increments, multiple flat-screen televisions, multiple computers, suites of furniture; it's mind-boggling! We took the evidence back to the office, and by Sunday, we'd identified over $600,000 in questionable spends in a period of less than twelve months. Up to this point, we'd been dealing with the CFO who'd brought us the case because her boss, the CEO, was out of town. Now he was back, and we called him with the news.

We had discovered that this administrative assistant had taken out multiple credit cards on the company account. Remember, this was a business with literally seventy different companies under its umbrella. Each of the companies has its own banking information and its own credit card information. A lot of regional banks have specialized divisions that deal with high-net-worth individuals; this is referred to as private banking. The goal of private banking groups is to get the accounts of high-net-worth individuals who have a lot of different businesses, such as our client. The private-banking people strive to become enmeshed in and an integral part of that person's life. The problem which leads to a lot of these private banks getting defrauded is that most of these wealthy investors have assistants who end up handling a lot of the transactions: "Mary, call so and so over at 'XYZ' bank and have them transfer $200,000 from this account to that account."

That's how the embezzling admin in question had gotten her fingers on the cash. When we looked at the email histories between the fraudster and the private bank, we could see she started out very slowly, getting to know the private banking rep she worked with very well, building up trust and a relationship. That way, when she initially told him, "John's too busy to talk with you, but you'll see we are deficient in this account. We need to transfer $200 from this other account to cover that deficiency. I'll send you a request in an email; please confirm." He didn't question it. Slowly, over a period of about six months she built up her credibility—and she used some pretty crafty methods, too. For instance, creating a fake email account for her boss, the CEO, so that "he" could see and respond to emails he'd never actually seen. She created the account using a variant of his actual email address, close enough that it slipped right past the bankers, who started using it as his address when they'd send notifications.

Within six months, those little $200 transfers had ballooned into $100,000 transfers. She'd discovered the weaknesses in the system and had figured out that she could create her own credit cards in her own name under these various accounts. When the credit cards would get a heavy bill, she would transfer money from one of his other accounts to pay off that credit card account. She knew that in the confusion of all these funds moving around it would take some time for the CFO and the accountants to find the leak and plug it. Imagine the difficulty of trying to find a charge for five Southwest gift cards in one of seventy companies, a year after it occurred! When you're going back through reconciling the books and you ask where the backup receipts are, a lot of companies, especially small ones, aren't that well organized. She knew that; she counted on them being understaffed and unlikely to notice these charges.

You may well wonder how someone could steal tens and hundreds of thousands of dollars without getting caught; certainly, if someone stole $1,000 from me, I'd know it. But if I'm running seventy different companies in a complex matrix, it can happen, and it does happen. Look at a company like Berkshire Hathaway; you're talking about tens of billions of dollars in assets, yet their total corporate staff is probably fewer than fifty people. It makes it possible for fraudsters like this admin to socially engineer relationships with useful people at the private bank, to take cards out on multiple businesses, and to shell game the cash flow.

It was a huge undertaking; we realized by Sunday that we were looking at fifteen to twenty different credit card accounts that had been opened, manipulations between twenty to thirty different business accounts, and fraudulent spending that had occurred over a three-year period. Clearly, this wasn't a mess we could clean up by Monday; this was going to be a process that would take many months just to tally up the damage and document it. Obviously, the client didn't want this woman on the job anymore, and he was also eager that she should face criminal charges.

Now, we enter into a different realm. It turns out that a white-collar event like this is not the easiest thing in the world for a police department to deal with. I don't care if it's a major police department like Houston or New York or Chicago or Los Angeles; police departments in today's world are just now getting traction on how to deal with white-collar embezzlement cases. Historically, this kind of thing has fallen more in the federal realm, with the FBI taking on cases that typically involved tens of millions of dollars being stolen by the Bernie Madoffs of the world.

But in the smaller world, if your controller writes a couple fraudulent checks, and you try to get that prosecuted criminally, good luck. Because it's a business transaction involving a person in your business, law enforcement oftentimes will see that as civil issue, not as a criminal issue. I disagree with that assessment. When someone works for you and writes a check for $10,000 for materials that are not used in your business or steals them from your loading dock when they come in, it's theft. Most police departments are used to dealing with blue-collar theft, so if I break into the storage facility in the middle of the night and take a pallet of cigarettes, they get that case. On the other hand, if I am the controller working for the cigarette distributor, and I create a fake vendor and siphon off $7,000 in false invoices and payments to a non-existent cleaning contractor, the police are going to have a hard time understanding that.

In this case, we had clear evidence that this administrative assistant made unauthorized transactions that were personally benefiting her; she'd ordered all this stuff and knew it was being shipped to her house. You'd think for a minute you could call the police and say, "This woman is stealing from me," and they would come in and do the computer forensic work and would actively take on the investigation and prosecution of the case. Wrong; they will not do that, because they don't have the manpower or the skills to do it. If you want this case prosecuted, the only way you're going to get their cooperation is by having a certified investigator and fraud examiner package up the materials to present to law enforcement.

We first met the suspected embezzler face to face that Monday afternoon when she came to work. We set up in the conference room, and she was called away from her desk to join me there, where I was sitting with one of the client's attorneys. Once she was seated, I introduced myself and told her, "I'm here investigating an allegation of you taking money from the company." As soon as she heard that, her face shifted in an almost frightening way; the visceral reaction, the rapidness of the blushing, the dilation of her pupils, the intensity of the swallowing, the immediate burst of perspiration were off the charts. You could literally feel this person's energy coming out of her and see that she had always known that this moment was going to come. In most of the embezzlement cases that I've worked, they're never shocked when you end up catching them. It's almost like they're shocked that they got away with it as long as they did. They know that there's evidence all over the place. It's not like they stole one or two checks three years ago and the money was wired out of the country and who the hell even remembers what this SB34X valve was for that no one remembers ordering or receiving? Just an error you write off.

But there was a huge paper trail that followed this person's hog path. Her slop pile was all over the damn place, and she knew it. She started hyperventilating, her eyes darting all over the room.

I lean in; "You need to listen to me. Calm down."

She said, "Are you arresting me?"

"I'm not a police officer, I don't have any power to arrest. I'm an investigator." I said, "But I do know what you've done. We imaged your computers, and I've seen all the orders that you placed with Amazon. I know about the thousand services of coffee. I know you chartered a private jet for you and your family." (She had chartered a plane for her and all of her "colorful" family members to go to their parents' fiftieth wedding anniversary in Pennsylvania—a $50,000 tab).

I wanted her to know that I knew the minute details, so there was no way to bullshit me. I said, "I even know what you ordered for lunch on the plane." This is the weird thing when you get into these cases; there are always these quirky little things that these embezzlers and fraudsters do to try to tamp down their guilt or provide some self-justification. Usually, for instance, when a person flies on a private plane, the food service is typically over-the-top decadent; cracked crab and shrimp and lobster and *foie gras*—all the things that you'd imagine. But this woman didn't do that; instead, she ordered Subway sandwiches for the whole family. She later said she wanted to save her boss money.

So I went over all this with her, and at this point I realized that she was about to projectile vomit on me, because she was hyperventilating so hard. It wouldn't be the first time, either: not my favorite part of the job by a long shot. She blurted out, "I've got to go to the bathroom!" and ran out of the office to the ladies' room where I could hear the retching from down the hall.

After about fifteen minutes I got worried that she was going to kill herself in there, so I got one of the female workers to go with me and went in. I said, "You need to get it together. Splash some water on your face."

By now she was crying; "I didn't mean to do anything. I love John!" Remember, she'd been running this confidence sting on her boss, John, for three years. She knew his wife, knew his kids, had been in his house when he was out of town. She'd looked after his dogs. You're talking about someone who knew everything about this guy. "I just wanted a better life for my family!"

I said, "Why don't you come talk to me about that?" She got control of herself and came back to the conference room.

At this point, some investigators would take a hard-nosed approach to try and get her to admit what she'd done. That's not how I roll. Excluding pedophiles, I'm able to summon up enough empathy for the person I'm interviewing to have a conversation that doesn't include me verbally waterboarding a person in order to get a confession. First, I actually respect the skill that it takes to do what she's done for three years. It's providing me with an opportunity to learn. Second, I don't fully understand how the person has gotten to this point in her life—and what I learned from working in mental hospitals is that when you take a more empathetic and understanding approach, people are more likely to open up. Ultimately we ended up with two videotaped discussions: one that day and one a week later in which she freely discussed everything she'd done and how she'd done it.

And, not surprisingly, this wasn't her first time at the rodeo. She had no criminal history, but she had been sued by past employers in civil court over allegations of embezzlement, which her current employer hadn't discovered when he ran her background check.

These checks, contrary to what you read in their marketing pitches, do a very poor job at reviewing civil court filings, which is how most of these cases are adjudicated since law enforcement is slack in getting involved. References? Yeah, she had a few, including her sister; interestingly, the sister too was a convicted fraudster.

At the end of the day, she'd burned through about a million dollars, and there wasn't a dime of it left. It was all spent on consumer items, on vacations, on school payments, and on paying her nieces' and nephews' auto insurance and car payments. She had played the role of a wealthy, benevolent matriarch to her family to the hilt—all with stolen money.

It took us about a month to reconstruct the case in a nice neat package to hand over to law enforcement. It included forensic images of her computer, videotaped confessions, details of receipts, and extensive email and texting histories. It took them a year to go over it and check it out, but she was finally indicted, and is, at this writing, looking at a long stay at Club Fed, probably four to ten for embezzlement, wire fraud, etc.

And she doesn't even have the money to pay for an attorney.

A few thoughts stay with me on this case. The client company was smart in that when they had an indication that something was seriously amiss with this admin, they turned to a professional to help gather digital evidence while it was still available. The understandable desire to have your existing IT support person or company that's not licensed as a forensic examiner do this risks contaminating the evidence and making it unusable in court. The same is true with getting a recorded confession; trying a "do-it-yourself" approach to a real issue is a mistake. The weight of your own testimony in court versus that of an outside licensed party makes the expense worth incurring, especially if you are going to seek a real criminal conviction or meaningful civil recovery.

If you want to pursue criminal actions against someone in a case like this, it's really best to have a professional company help you package up the materials before you present the case to law enforcement. These cases can be complex, and most local law enforcement agencies don't have the resources to chase suspected embezzlers. Again, do not imagine that your local PD has forensic accountants on staff standing at the ready to do your work for you. The more prepared and straightforward your case is, the better your chances are that they will pay attention to it. This means all the receipts, bank records, etc. Law enforcement will have to independently recreate all the work that you have done, so what you are doing is creating an easy-to-follow guide for them. The easier the guide, the more likely they are to take the case. Why can't they just use your work product? The short answer concerns rules of evidence. They do this in order to have a unique record of the fraud material directly from the sources via subpoena. This is designed to independently gather evidence outside of material provided by the victim.

Finally, you can get more out of someone with an empathetic approach to an interview than with a hard-ass approach. It's important to note that the empathy cannot be disingenuous; people can read insincerity. Find a place from which you can try to understand a person's viewpoint, however distorted it may be. They often want you to understand that they are not a bad person but rather just a "good person" in a bad situation who made some bad decisions. Using this empathic conversational approach can be a real opportunity to gain insight.

CHAPTER FIVE

YOU CAN GET ANYTHING ON THE INTERNET

You're probably pretty familiar with the Internet—but have you heard about the Dark Net? When you read about the areas on the Internet where drugs are transacted, human trafficking is done, arms deals are brokered, or hackers are hired—that's the Dark Net.

One step removed from the darkest of the Dark Net is what we call the Gray Net: sites that exist to connect the buyers and sellers of sexual services. We are not talking about kiddie porn or human trafficking here; the services offered are mostly illegal but a far cry from the Dark Net world of the truly horrible. They're activities between consenting adults that most modern libertarians would argue should be legal. What they're selling is everything from twenty-something-year-old college females looking to make a little extra money, targeting the thirty-plus adult male population, to married people looking to have anonymous affairs. Websites like AshleyMadison. com exist specifically to enable extramarital or outside relationships. They're designed to be covert. And then one click over from that are specialty sites, those that cater to more specific appetites.

Ten or more years ago, if you were into BDSM (bondage/sado-masochism), or you were a rubberist, or you liked to dress up in girls' clothes and have someone degrade you, it was more difficult to find purveyors of those services. Sometimes they were listed in the back of whatever local magazine covered your area. Maybe it was an online billboard. Maybe you knew someone who worked at a strip club who knew someone that did specialty services. But in today's world, a few strokes of the Internet and you can tap into the Gray Net and find these fetishes repackaged as consumer services.

The man who would become my client knew his way around the Gray Net. A successful lawyer, in his midfifties, divorced, and a familiar figure in the community, he had developed a serious porn addiction over the course of five years. One of the things that I'll always tell clients is that they need to tell me exactly the situation that they're involved in, every part of it. And they don't need to feel uncomfortable or ashamed talking to me. There are a few exceptions: If the case involves sexual relations with underaged children, not only do I not want to know, but if they tell me, I'm going to refer them to the criminal authorities, because that's not something that we do or deal with. And if they're involved in human trafficking or narcotics trafficking, they'd better not tell me, because I will refer them to the police also. We have never been, nor will we ever be, involved in anything related to that.

Quite honestly, I don't care what happens to people like that. Remember, when you talk to an investigator like me, you really need someone to help you handle your bad situation. *Unless you fully explain to me how bad it is, I can't begin to develop a strategy or a plan to help extricate you from it.* Most people realize pretty quickly when they start talking to me that this is probably not the first time I've had this kind of conversation. I don't even blush, and most of the time you really wouldn't see any reflection on my face, because the fact is, it's rare that I actually hear something that I've never dealt with or seen before.

But it became very clear when I initially talked to this client that he was a little embarrassed. A guy like him is the last person most people would see as someone likely to resort to the Internet for sex. He's enviable; well off, good-looking, seemingly positioned to enjoy the full cornucopia of possible relationships. But in my experience, things aren't always what they appear. In my experience, the people who go through these traumas are oftentimes in material states of despair and very often suffering from clinical depression. It's a difficult spot for guys like this to trust in new relationships; is it him she likes or his money? Sometimes—and certainly for this guy—watching porn may seem a lot easier and cleaner. But after three or four years of it, the basic vanilla porn just didn't do it for him anymore: not even the more exotic offerings on porn sites like Redtube, and those can get pretty exotic by most people's standards, ranging from domination scenarios to aggressive rape scenarios. What you find is that someone who's on that slippery slope, trying to find continued stimulation, can pretty quickly find themselves on the other side and into the Gray Net, potentially even to the Dark Net.

That's what happened to this guy; he got into a particular flavor of BDSM where he enjoyed having others degrade him. So he went shopping for a dominatrix on Alt.com, a sex-market website that has listings of specialists who are consumer-reviewed, just like you would find on Yelp. Say I want to find an African American woman who is good at kicking someone in the balls; you'll find her there, and she's got reviews: how she did it, what her price points were. If you wanted her to step on your penis with her high heels, what's the markup for that? Was she too hard? Was she too soft? Would she swear at you? Did she do an in-call? Did she do an out-call? Every variation you could imagine is on there. So our guy made the leap from masturbating to BDSM porn to trying to figure out if he could actually get it done in person, and he jumped into the world of the alt.coms, seeking an arrangement.

But because this guy in particular had a higher profile, he was nervous about actually contracting someone, fearful that they would recognize his face or connect the dots to his identity. He was terrified that his children would find out that he was into what he defined as deviant sexual behavior. Finally, he found a dominatrix on an online site who'd interact with him virtually. He wanted her to make demands, to give him orders to obey; If the dominatrix says, "Slap your dick on the desk," he slaps his dick on the desk. If she says, "Call yourself a fat fucking pig," he has to call himself a fat fucking pig. There's a particular type of online dominatrix I refer to as an ATM dominatrix, which means that she likes to punish her clients financially, so she will withhold the act.

The guy will say, "Please dominatrix, let me touch my cock."

"No, you fat fucking worthless pig. I'm not going to let you touch your cock and balls. You have to pay your dominatrix $100, you filthy rich, stupid fucking cocksucker. You send me the money now, and if you do, I'll let you touch your pathetic small dick."

"Yes, dominatrix, I'm sorry I didn't pay you enough last time. I'm going to pay you $200 this time."

"I didn't say for you to pay me $200 this time, you fat fucking slob. I told you $100. You think you can buy everyone with your money? You can't buy me. I'm not going to talk to you anymore today. Put your small dick back in your fucking pants and don't call me again."

That was the kind of deal this guy got into. In time, he found his ideal woman on Alt.com: six foot one, black hair, huge breasts and nipples, shiny black boots, the whole nine yards. She was a tough-looking alpha female, sort of your classic German S&M porn type. He basically engaged her and started a regular online thing, paying her every time. This guy was worth millions, so spending $500 or $1,000 a session wasn't all that consequential to him. They began with her emailing him photos of herself in her full regalia, and there were tons of highly graphic language between them and not a whole lot of small talk. It wasn't, "How was your morning?" It was all fairly directly to the point.

So one time she said, "I want you to send me toys," because he eventually wanted to progress to having her do things he wanted and transition from the virtual to the real. He sent some sex toys to an address she gave him in California. It was evident in some of the communications that he started opening up a bit, talking about where he was from. He'd been using a false name in his emails, but he hadn't realized that he was sending his email through a normal email exchange, which showed the IP address and by default the section of the city that he was from.

Slowly, gradually, the dominatrix was socially engineering him into feeling more comfortable. Of course, he was being worked the whole time. This took place over a period of a few weeks, probably when he first started talking to the dominatrix. Every time he wouldn't respond to her quickly enough, she would email in capital letters the word B-U-Z-Z, as if to shock him: "You fat bastard, you're not responding to me quick enough. Buzz, buzz, buzz, buzz, buzz." After about a month, he was communicating with this person three different ways: email, email chat, and phone texting. Because of all that, by the time they *really* started escalating things on him and took it to the next step, they had a fairly good idea of his geography based on the IP addresses from his email. They knew his phone number. They knew his name. They tracked down his Facebook account, and they knew his entire social network.

Eventually she got him to send some photos of himself and then moved him along to doing some video chatting. That's where these cases always go, from the virtual to the real. But in the case of extortion (and that's where this was going), there's a different goal because the extorter's never going to actually physically meet the victim. What the extorter is going to do is gather enough information about you so that when they demand money from you, you feel as though you've been fully duped. You've exposed the worst parts of yourself—literally—both physically and mentally, and you're really at the person's mercy.

She got him to start video chatting. This guy was into pinning, which is where you take clothespins and clip them to various parts of your body. In the pictures that he sent, there were clothespins on his testicles, on his penis, and on his nipples; there were clothespins around his anus and on the insides of his thighs. She got him worked up over a couple of hours, and by the end of that time, this guy was sitting there, buck naked, with twenty clothespins all over his penis, balls, anus, and breasts, with a glassy look in his eyes. The dominatrix now had full video and photographs of him saying all kinds of things from "Fuck me in the ass" to insulting racial slurs. In that two hours they'd covered nearly every embarrassing, degrading thing that one human could possibly say. If this video became public, the guy's very public career would be unrecoverable.

I was called into this case by a senior partner at his firm whom the victim had confided in. The man who called me had known this guy his whole life, known he'd gone through a difficult divorce, and knew that his friend was into some kind of weird shit. He just didn't know it had all spun this far out of control. He also knew that this guy was a huge earner, and it would be damaging to everyone if this came out, so he called me on a Friday evening at around 5:30, when I was in traffic going home.

I was in the victim's living room two hours later, where he told me all the above details. After about three hours, I realized he was in really a very bad spot. He'd done two or three video sessions with the dominatrix, with the clothespins and the racial slurs and every version of human sexual experience, from hetero to homo to trans to … I mean, some of it, even *I* had to look up in a reference manual.

The reason he had panicked enough to tell his partner about it all was that they'd sent him an email, in which they used his full name, referenced his Facebook page, and included a list of about seventy-five of his family and friends and colleagues, complete with their emails and even their phone numbers. The message was, "You disgusting pig. You're going to pay me what I ask, and if you don't, we're going to share your real world with all of your friends and family."

He panicked and started paying; within two weeks, about the time it took him to tell his friend about it, he was already out $25,000, with no end in sight. The only reason they weren't bleeding him faster was that the extorter wanted it sent via MoneyGram, and there are limits on how much you can send that way at one time.

By the time I saw him, he was a wreck; he hadn't slept for almost a week, hadn't gone into work and was in very bad shape. He showed me the videos, showed me the photos, showed me the whole email exchange: everything. Intelligently, he had kept all the receipts of the money he had sent and where he had sent it, plus all his communications.

The first thing I asked him was, "Do you think you know this person? Is there anything that would give you an indication that you knew this person?"

"No."

"How did you find the person?"

"I met her on Alt.com."

"Well, how did you find your way into Alt.com?" I asked, because that's not just a site that an average person would know about.

"Well, I started off with Ashley Madison, and I got on to Secret Arrangements, and then I got on to ..."

This was important to me because I'm always profiling. I'm profiling not only the potential perpetrator, but I also have to profile my client, because when my client's talking to me, I have to assume a couple of things. One, there's probably a few things he's not telling me that are important for me to know. And on a rare occasion, I get a client who I don't want to work with. Everyone's a little worse than they seem, but I have to be careful that they're not a whole lot worse than they seem. I don't want to get into a case with a guy and find out that this guy's into kiddy porn or something, because I'm going to flip on him immediately. So I asked the guy how he found a site like that to get an indication of where he was coming from. It became clear to me that he had not been into the scene to this degree for very long before getting nailed by an extortionist.

The traditional piece of the investigation involved getting the full download from the client, understanding the exact issue, and understanding his past. The cyber piece was examining the digital evidence that we had. We forensically imaged his computer. We forensically imaged his phone. I got to know this guy's background, including the language and the terms that he used, well enough that I was able to impersonate him in texting with the extortionist. The guy couldn't handle it anymore, so I took possession of his cell phone.

When you do detailed analysis of email, in the metadata of the emails, you can determine the IP address from which the email was sent. In this particular case, some of the emails were coming from an IP address near San Francisco, from what's called a "static" IP. With a lot of bigger bandwidth IT providers, you'll have a static IP address. Oh the other hand, if you're at your house, your Internet rotates your IP address as your router resets itself. I get one of your emails from home, I can tell you generally the area you live in, within maybe 50 miles—but that's not really going to tell me very much. However, if you had a static IP address, I could potentially track you right down to the building you're in. In this case, we were able to narrow it down to a specific house.

We determined who lived in that house, and we put it under surveillance. I was communicating with this dominatrix, and honestly, it was a weird communication. You had to ignore the extortion going on, because the dominatrix didn't really want you to focus on the extortion. The dominatrix, in essence, said, "We know who you are. You're going to pay." But the dominatrix never said, "You're going to pay me $100,000." She never said, "You're going to pay me a million." She just said, "You're going to pay." I felt that they were hoping to keep this "relationship" going over a long term. When I'd bring up the emails that were going to reach out to everyone he knew and basically burn him to the ground, she would say, "I don't want to talk about that now. I want to talk about your pathetic shriveled cock." And she'd order him to send her another $200.

That pattern was good for us, because if we could track these little bits of money, we had a better chance to see who was getting them. As I said, we'd put the house under surveillance; the person demanded a few payments, and we sent them. And sure as hell, as she demanded the money, and we paid it, we saw a person come out of the house and head right to the MoneyGram store; the person stayed at the store for a little while, then came out, got back in the car, and drove back to the house. During a week's surveillance, this person almost never left the house except after we sent money. And it turned out that the person who was leaving the house was a twenty-two-year-old white male! He looked like a fat surfer, who was living with his parents. Not a down-and-out family by any means; this was a $600K home and a solid white-collar family—whose son happened to be in the extortion business. We got his license plate and his photograph, and I've got guys on the ground there, so we ran his background. The guy had no background at all. Nothing—just a nobody. He looked like some kid who'd spent his years playing World of Warcraft. And it didn't make any sense to us.

We finally decided that we were going to confront the kid and find out what his story was. We found his cell phone number on one of our databases, and I called him on his phone. I knew his name. I knew everything about him.

I said, "Listen, this extortion that you've been involved in, it turns out that you're extorting the wrong guy. This guy is a very well-connected, powerful guy. And you need to tell me everything that's going on; you need to agree to let us come to your house and remove all this information off of your computer. And you're going to be signing some non-disclosure agreements. I'm going to assume right now that this is just a big miscommunication. But if it's not a miscommunication, and it turns out that you really were involved in a material extortion, you could be looking at a referral to local law enforcement, and this could end up being very bad for you."

Of course, the guy completely freaked out on the phone to me. And what he told me actually surprised me; it turned out that he had also been a victim and got caught up in a similar situation. He'd gotten involved in a homoerotic online relationship that followed almost the exact same pattern of what he did to our client. He had shared video sessions online, with him engaging in homoerotic acts that included the use of sex toys in his rectum. His extortionist did the exact same thing. He was told, "We know your friends and your family and all the Facebook information," exactly as *he* had done with my client. "And if you don't send us money, we're going to send these images of you calling out some guy's name and pushing a dildo in your ass to all your friends and family."

So the guy forked out what little bit of money he had, but that was only a couple grand. And once they burned through his money, they told him, "You're going to help us with other victims that we're generating. Sometimes you're going to help us with emails, and sometimes you're going to pick up money for us at this MoneyGram store, and you're going to send it to us in Nigeria." The masterminds behind this whole thing were part of a Nigerian extortion ring, and this ring was working scores of people in exactly the same scenario that we've discussed. We determined that the money was in fact going to Nigeria, because we would send him the MoneyGram, he would cash the MoneyGram, and he would immediately send the money via MoneyGram from the same store to an office in Lagos, Nigeria.

Going forward, we had two issues. I felt it was highly likely that some of this information would come out on our client; that once we spun it out, the Nigerians basically would have nothing to lose, and they could burn our client. The second issue was how to keep these people from continuing to extort our client.

We did two things. First, we called a meeting of our client and his closest friends. We said, "Your friend is a victim of an extortion campaign. We think that it's coming from an old, scorned girlfriend, someone we think has probably developed a drug problem and now has acquired a new degenerate drug-addict sponsor." We told them that there were some bogus, manipulated photos of their friend out there, and to show them how it could be done, we passed around some doctored photos of their friend that we'd mocked up. We have some great photo-editing people on our team, so we took some pictures of the client and gave him a series of interesting makeovers to prove our point: "Here's a picture of your friend, and here's a picture of your friend with no pants on. And here's a picture of your friend with no shirt on with a tattoo of a dragon on his chest. And here's a picture of your friend with a Mohawk."

Now, if you know what you're doing with Photoshop, there are ways to spot if a picture's been altered or not, but to the average eye, it's hard to know without a forensic analysis. I was banking on this group not having that level of expertise—so we told his friends and family this: "Your friend is getting extorted, and you may be seeing some disturbing things about your friend, images that are faked like these are."

Now, some people might take issue with the idea of us lying like this to the friends and family, but to me, the bigger issue was that my client had been extorted over something that wasn't illegal and was in fact his personal business. And on principle, I felt it was wrong. That's why I felt no guilt over crafting a scenario that easily could have been true.

We did this before we contacted the extortionists because we were pretty sure they'd retaliate by dumping this guy's photos as they'd threatened. So for about a two-week period, I'd been going back and forth with the dominatrix, and if I didn't answer my phone quick enough, she texted me, "Buzz, buzz, buzz." And it was really very weird; sometimes in this business, you're sitting there having lunch with someone, and they ask, "Who are you texting?" Of course, you really can't fully explain to them what exactly you're dealing with at that very moment in time. Or you're having dinner with your kids, and you can't really explain to them that Thunder, the Nigerian dominatrix extortionist, is sending text versions of electrocution over my client's cell phone because they're upset that I haven't sent them enough money.

I ended up sending an email to the extortionist: "This is who we are, this is our firm, this is what I've been communicating with you about for the last two weeks. We know that you've been extorting this person; here's the record of the money that we've sent you. I suggest that you go find a new victim because this hole is tapped out, and his friends and family already know about it. There's nothing you can do to hurt the guy, and all it's going to do is basically bring a lot of unwelcome attention to you and hurt your business. Go away."

And it worked. They disappeared.

This worked because we'd backstopped the extortion by coming up with a plausible explanation for whatever the extortionists might throw at the friends and family by using photo manipulation to show what could be done with an innocent photograph. If they had seen those actual photos, would they have suspected there might be something to it? Probably. Would they have doubted it? Yes, they would have doubted it—and planting that seed of doubt was enough to protect our client.

For me, this underscores the fact that most criminal activity of this type is not malicious. It's business. Once the perpetrators finally realize that the play is played out, they know enough not to really burn the guy. Because if the story made it to the local and national news, then other victims would know about the scam and avoid it.

Scams like this that are run on the Gray Net and the Dark Net tend to work because the people involved are in the shadows, and they don't want light shined on them. We look at the profile of the victim and the perpetrator and at the economic model of the crime. If the economic model of the crime is "scared victim/gaining perpetrator" then without a scared victim, the perpetrator doesn't have any leverage. And the perpetrator doesn't want to be known beyond the few people being extorted.

My client was a happy man. I hope for his sake he's not a repeat client. What did we learn—other than online BDSM extortionists like to text the word "buzz"? We learned that without the digital capabilities to discover the perpetrators' IP addresses, we couldn't have brought this case to a safe conclusion for the client. Using that digital evidence in a traditional interview yielded additional information that made it possible to trace the money orders. Without those digital skills, our client would still be on the hook.

And, lastly, we learned how useful a good photo doctor can be when trying to out-game Nigerian extortionists.

CHAPTER SIX

EVERY STEP YOU TAKE: CYBERSTALKING

Another class of criminal whose work has been made much easier by modern technology is the stalker, today more likely to be a cyberstalker. What do we mean by stalker? Generally, it's someone who borders on a compulsion to observe, influence, and control the object of his or her interest or desire. It could be your soon-to-be ex-wife or ex-husband or your ex-lover; as it happens, in most of the cases we work, the women are our clients and the men are the alleged stalkers. We've worked with people where it was the other way around, but that's fairly unusual; in five years I've maybe had one such case.

Typically, I get a call from a woman who's extremely distraught, verging on hysterical, so much so that it's hard to be sure the person calling isn't mentally ill herself. What she's saying is always the same; "He's hacking my phone, he's hacking my network, he's hacking my wireless system; he's got people following me." The kinds of claims that really make you wonder about her sanity are things like, "He's coming into my apartment and moving things around."

From my perspective, cyberstalking is interesting because it combines two areas in which I've spent most of my professional life. In my early adult life, I worked in the psychotic disorders unit of a mental hospital, with a group that was mostly bipolar and had psychotic episodes. I spent significant time in graduate school studying that particular topic, and I got very good at hearing the disorder lurking behind the words. But with my investigator's ear, I'm hearing something that may actually have a basis in fact, and if so, what are the facts associated with it?

The first thing I always do when listening to these cases is to get clear on why this would or could be happening. If the person's going through divorce, there are a lot of potential benefits to cyberstalking somebody, even when the issue is not a pathological one, where the person becomes obsessed with the idea that his soon-to-be ex-wife has got a new man. If there are child custody or financial issues at stake, having the ability to intercept communications between someone and his or her attorney, family, or investigator actually is a worthwhile thing to do. It gives the stalker the upper hand, which is the reason people have been wiretapping and eavesdropping since the beginning of time. Especially now, in the cyber world in which we live, where most people communicate via cell phones, texts, and email. The software available to do the eavesdropping is extremely easy to procure and very inexpensive, and it's extremely difficult to track who has put it in and who is benefitting from that illegal digital information.

For example: You call me and tell me that you think your phone is compromised. I get the phone and I run software through our mobile forensic lab, which shows me that, yes, there is spyware on your phone. Spyware and the receiver of the information is not a one-to-one relationship, so it's not like I can tie that IP address down to who's observing it. The information goes from the mobile phone to a server, and then the viewer of the information dials into that server from a laptop or some other type of device. You can't see who's looking at that information, and it's designed that way. If I put spyware on your laptop, the spyware would be gathering what you're doing, close to real-time, and it would be pushing it to a server.

Typically these servers are located offshore. I would go to my laptop, dial in, and I would view the server it was being gathered on. Thus, there's one connection between your computer and the server offshore and another connection between my computer that's viewing it and the server offshore, and those two paths do not meet. It's not a triangle or a straight line; it's a V that is designed not to be easy to decipher. If you think that an offshore Singapore rack-mounted server owned by a Chinese spyware company is going to give up an IP address because of an American subpoena, you're wrong.

People who are being spied on typically say, "I want to prove that it's him doing it, and I want to nail him," because usually the stalking begins *after* the initial orders are put in in a divorce. Once the temporary orders are put in, it's difficult to say, "Well, it was a joint asset, and I have the rights to monitor communications." There's an expectation of privacy between a person and her lawyer that's nearly a sacred value in this country. If you find out your soon-to-be ex is monitoring your communications, that's going to be a very big issue if you can prove it in court. It can even be a criminal referral issue, because eavesdropping in that area of post-orders is illegal and violates all manner of federal wiretapping rules.

A woman who found herself in this position came into my office after a brief and clearly uncomfortable conversation on the phone, in which she revealed that she suspected her ex of hacking her computer. She'd gone online and scared the bejesus out of herself reading stuff on the Internet about all the ways her husband could be watching her, most of which is bullshit.

For instance, they say it is possible to remotely install spyware on smartphones, but that's not so. If I wanted to bug your phone, I would have to have physical possession of your phone and download software physically onto your phone. Now, can the National Security Agency (NSA) do it? Probably. But honestly, they don't have to do it, because the government can monitor phone calls from the actual cell phone provider, so they don't need your phone. But your ex can't—even if he works in information technology.

This woman came in with five cell phones, convinced that all five of them had been compromised and that I was going to find evidence of spyware on them. I explained about the necessity of a bad guy having the phone in his actual possession to install spyware, and she told me that her spouse had been in her house up until a week previous. People don't understand about the necessity for physical possession of the phone, and they panic; they're out there buying "burner" phones by the handful, and as soon as they hear any odd little clicks or pops, they toss them. While we were sitting there, her phone went "beep-beep," and she wanted to toss it out the window.

The more I heard about her situation, the better I understood her paranoia. Her ex had installed software on her laptop and spyware on her phone in the past. He'd even put a GPS device on her vehicle.

All of the knowledge and equipment to accomplish this is on the Internet, and the cost is negligible. I'm not sure what had happened to turn him into a control freak maniac stalker and make him want to monitor her movements—but at the time, they were in the throes of a divorce, one of the most stressful life events anyone can endure, and she was cracking under the strain. It was almost as though she was suffering from post-traumatic stress disorder. She called me when she was coming to my office, saying, "He's got people following me again." The truth is, I'm a private investigator, and yes, people do get followed, so the fact is that sometimes such paranoia is justified. You can't just dismiss their claims out of hand.

When she'd finished telling me what she'd been experiencing, I said, "Okay. We're going to search your phones for spyware. Your observation is one data point to me, and it's a relevant one to me. It's the experience of an alleged victim. But it is only one data point. I have to independently verify what you're saying, so if I go to court on either a civil or criminal matter, I can say 'Yes, we witnessed this first-hand, and here is what we witnessed.'"

So we gathered up her phones and her laptop and started searching them for spyware. A few minutes of Internet research is all it takes to find mSpy and WebWatcher and Net Nanny and many other options for DIY stalkers—cheap, easy, and effective. Whether you're justifiably or non-justifiably paranoid, it will scare the shit out of you.

We've got a quarter of a million dollars invested in our forensic lab, so if there is spyware there, we most likely can find it. And if there *is* something on the phone, here's what we do: nothing. We actually leave it on the phone. Why? Well, if I'm going to prove that you're spying on me, how am I going to do it? I can't just say the software exists, because how can I prove that you installed it? Maybe I installed it to try to implicate you.

So instead of uninstalling the software or turning it over to the police, we start putting misinformation on the cell phone. Whatever stimulates the alleged stalker most is what we'll start putting on the cell phone. Say my soon-to-be ex-husband is fixated on the fact that I have a new boyfriend. In that case, I text the boyfriend on that phone. I'm a faithful heterosexual male, but I've been known to play various roles in texting with clients, so occasionally I'm a lesbian, a swinger, or whatever else is called for, and I'll use these texts to draw the stalker into coming out into the open to observe a "meeting." So we'll set a fake meeting at a weird time and a weird place; maybe I'll set a meeting at Barney's Burgers, down on nowhere road at 3 in the afternoon, and place my client there with a companion. If her stalker shows up to observe her, we're staked out across the street, and we'll record the person observing her. We'll do that two or three times to establish that this wasn't by chance—that the stalker knew where she'd be and when, which is knowledge he could only have gained by having access to her texts. Any judge in any court in the world would understand.

Now you've got something. From a court perspective, they're going to be extremely punitive because then the question becomes, "How long has that spyware been on that phone?" and typically we can determine that it's been on for at least six months. The assumption at that point is that the stalker has observed all the communications between the person and his or her attorney, investigators, and everyone else.

In my experience, though, it's rare even under these circumstances for the court to take punitive action because it's difficult to prove that it was in fact the stalker who installed the malware on the phone. You would not have a video recording of him installing it. He could claim that he was just following the victim. Maybe that's enough to get a restraining order, but it's just not enough for a criminal charge.

Now, how can you tell if a car has a tracking device? Well, you can buy a good-quality GPS device with a cellular signal online for about $500. I could monitor that in real time, and you would never know it was on your car. Unfortunately, the stuff you buy online that is supposed to let you check for these devices is useless. Professionals like us have the equipment to sweep a car properly, so if you suspect you're being tracked, you need a professional sweep to ascertain that.

What about your home … has the stalker actually installed a listening device in your house? Again, this is a very easy thing to buy and use. Miniaturized recording gear of extremely high quality is now available for well under a thousand dollars. I could easily go in your house and, in a short period of time, scatter around five or six different devices—and you wouldn't know they were there. They're motion-activated, and the battery packs last for a long time.

The transmission of the information offsite is a little more complicated, which means that retrieving the information is also more difficult; still, in cases like this woman's, we'll typically sweep the house for audio and video bugs. Even if we don't find anything, we can at least restore her sense of privacy. Now she knows her house is not bugged; we've removed the spyware off her phone, and we've installed some anti-spyware gear on it. We have updated her firewall and her IP security in her house. We've taken her from privacy intrusion to privacy protection, so now she's able to feel like she can have secured communications with her attorney, so she's a lot less stressed. It's almost like a Maslow's hierarchy of needs, where the top of the list is a sense of safety and security, and when that's violated, it has a rippling effect in people. Typically, a guy who becomes a stalker was abusive beforehand, so it's not a single incident; it may have been years of extreme behavior that culminated in this divorce. In the best-case scenario, we're able to testify in court to what happened, and things have a tendency to normalize.

A problem I've seen, though, is that these people may experience something that retriggers a memory of the privacy violation, and it re-stimulates the fear; in probably 40 percent of the cases, the client will call me back within a year, under the impression the spying is going on again. In most cases, it's not: The person doesn't have physical access to the devices, we've put in updated security firewalls, and unless the stalker is a former NSA engineer, he is honestly not going to be able to get around the kind of stuff we put in. But the fact is, this kind of personal violation takes a long time to recover from. It's sad, and sometimes clients become kind of angry with you. When someone thinks the conspiracy is going on, the only thing he or she really wants to hear is "yes, it is" and "I believe you," but that's not the business we're in. We're in the business of *can we prove it, and is it a defensible position?*

Once in a while, I'm startled when a victim's wild claims turn out to be true. Here's an extreme case I remember: A woman called me on the phone and told me a story about how she inherited money from her father and how she's been systematically defrauded over time to the tune of two and a half million dollars via identity theft. Sometimes, when you hear these really crazy stories, it's originating from the person's sibling or parent, which still amazes me every time. Now, my family life when I was growing up wasn't the most apple-pie experience, but my family stopped well short of stealing from each other, so I was more than a little dubious. Still, she insisted her sister was stealing from her, so I ran a background check on her sister—nothing. But I did find someone who was sharing the sister's address—her boyfriend. Bingo! The guy proved to be a legendary identity thief, a well-known multiple offender who'd served time for organized crime charges under the RICO (Racketeer Influenced and Corrupt Organizations) act. You know the kind of person you have to be for the feds to charge you with the RICO statute on identity theft? You have to be the Tony Soprano of the identity theft world. So I realized, "Holy Shit! This woman's story is real!" She was being robbed systematically by her sister's boyfriend.

A few concluding thoughts: Keep an open mind. Consider why someone would be stalking your client; what do they have to gain? If it's a divorce, that's an easy answer, especially if money or kids are at stake. Sometimes the paranoid *are* being followed.

The comments and experiences of the client are one data point, but that data point may honestly be somewhat distorted. You have to listen to it, you have to digest it; there's certainly something in it, even if you don't know exactly what that is.

Make sure you have a competent computer-forensic or mobile-forensic expert examine the devices. There is no easy way to do that, and traditional PIs, or even IT people, are not experts in that area. Many states require that the investigation be performed by a certified computer-forensic examiner, who typically also has to be a licensed private investigator. So from a consumer standpoint, you really want to make sure that's who you're working with.

Another lesson would be the importance of re-establishing a sense of privacy with the client. You need to understand how deeply the client believes her privacy's been violated and come up with a plan to help her re-establish a sense of privacy, whether it requires a legitimate bug sweep of the house or sweeping the car or checking her new boyfriend's cell phone. It's important to do this with a client, because until people have re-established a sense of privacy, they don't function well. Most investigators don't have a background in therapy, and despite my attempt to get out of psychology, I still find those skills get called on, especially in cases like these.

I don't like seeing people suffer. I guess ultimately people like me get into this line of work because we have a protective nature. But divorces are highly contentious, and there are often multiple reasons for trying to gain an upper hand, whether it's for legal or financial or psychological reasons. It's a continuation of whatever pathological issues were in the relationship to begin with, and technology now makes it easy for an emotionally fraught condition to become even worse. It's almost too tempting to the person who wants to do it, so they cross the line because they can.

As I'm writing this book, I have four cyberstalking cases—and if I played you the tapes of these women telling their stories, you'd swear it was the same person talking on each one. That's how similar these kinds of cases are and how widespread the problem of cyberstalking has become. My goal is to end my clients' uncertainty, to secure their privacy, and to help them on the path to getting past the stresses of their divorce.

CHAPTER SEVEN

SPARKLE PONY IN THE BARN

The story of this case begins, as many of them do in my business, with someone calling me on the phone to say they think their spouse has someone on the side. Seventy percent of the time, that call comes from a woman, and this particular case started with that traditional call—a heterosexual woman calling in about her husband. She was in her midforties; her husband was in his late-forties, early-fifties. She said, "I think my husband is having an affair."

Typically, I'll ask, "Why do you think that?" Usually, the person will say something along the lines of, "There's been an emotional distance between us over a period of time. He's been traveling a lot. It's been a number of months since we've had any sexual contact." These days, the laundry list usually includes, "He's always on his phone or on his computer."

I'll say, "Well, first, are you actually legally married?" because that is a relevant question that impacts what we do going forward: "Do you own your vehicles together, making them a marital asset? Or is a vehicle a business asset?" If the vehicle is a marital asset, then we try to GPS the vehicle. In cases like this, we verify the title ownership of the car and send someone out in the middle of the night to slip up under the car and attach a GPS device. Typically, these devices have a heavy magnetic case that locks up to the metal undercarriage of the car. That allows us to track the driver's movements in real time to see where he goes and how long he stays.

The second question we always ask is, "What type of phone does the person have?" If we know the type of phone and we can get access to it, we could forensically image that phone. Now, notice I didn't say we would bug the phone; I didn't say we'd put any kind of software in the phone to monitor communications, text messages, audio, etc. What we want to get is a forensic image of the phone. We ask the same question about that phone: "Is it a work asset, or is it a marital family asset?" If it's a work phone, the user doesn't always own the phone or the data on the phone, and there can be legal issues with copying information off the device. However, in today's world, most companies want people to bring in their own phones simply to avoid the cost. (This is a terrible idea, by the way; as the business owner, you have no control over the data on that phone, and you have no right to look at what's on it. If I'm stealing from you, as your employee, I'm typically going to be doing a lot of the nefarious communication around my crime on my phone—and if it's *my* phone, you can't look at it.)

As an example, here's how we'd go about forensically imaging an iPhone, which is the most common. When I send texts on my iPhone, even if I delete them, most of those deleted texts still exist on the phone. And if I do an iTunes backup of my phone on my computer, it actually also backs up all the stuff I've deleted. So if I can get the phone or a backup of the phone from a computer, I can forensically recover most of the information that's on that phone. What I can recover is pretty comprehensive, including the text messages plus a lot of the emails. It will show the websites that the person goes to. It will show all the times that the location services are on—where the phone has actually been.

Today, it's a safe bet that if someone under the age of seventy-five is doing something wrong, their phone is involved. In any nefarious behavior—from stealing employer secrets, to having an affair, to conducting criminal activity—that phone becomes the central repository of all of the related communication. So we definitely want to get access to the phone.

This lady's husband was an executive who ran a fairly large company based here in Texas, someone you would have recognized from the media, a guy whose face was on the company commercials. He kept his phone next to him at night—in his pillowcase, in fact—(always a bad sign) but his wife was able to get him a little liquored up one night and grabbed it after he was asleep. She knew his password, but when she had gone secretly onto the phone and looked, she didn't see anything, because he was deleting the texts. She snuck the phone out of the house to where we were waiting. We showed her how to back up the phone and created a copy of its contents. Now, there's nothing on the phone that reveals that it's been backed up; there's no trace of that. We also slapped a GPS on his car, which was marital property.

She had guessed that he was sleeping with his attractive, twenty-something administrative assistant. She was upset about it, but she sort of understood. She wasn't sure if she was going to use the information we might uncover for divorce filing. She wasn't 100 percent sure *what* she wanted to do with it.

One thing we tell clients when they're going through cases like this is that what's relevant for a divorce or potential divorce is wholly dependent on the state you live in. Some things matter in some states. In other states, those things don't matter. Some states let you GPS someone's car because it's a marital asset. Some states won't. In some states, one person can record a conversation. In other states, both parties have to acknowledge the recording, and violation of some of those laws can have some fairly dire consequences. You should always refer back to the privacy issues associated with the state in which you live. But in the great state of Texas, you can GPS an asset that you own, which makes sense. You can also look at a phone you own as a marital asset. And when you're thinking about should you or should you not do something to gather information, you should think carefully about why it is that you're doing it. Are you doing it to find out, "Is the person faithful to me?" with the thought that "If I find out the person is not faithful to me, I will file for a divorce"? Typically, in 90 percent of the cases we're involved in, that's what the client is thinking about.

So we ask the question, "What's relevant in a divorce?" In most parts of major metropolitan areas in Texas, the courts really don't care anymore about your spouse being involved in an affair. And they really don't care if someone smokes marijuana. What they care about is whether or not someone is engaged in high-risk behavior or whether or not someone lies about his or her assets. They also care about eavesdropping on the privileged communications between a person and his or her attorney or doctor. What qualifies as high-risk behavior are things like: "My husband's buying drugs. My husband's buying cocaine. My husband has been smoking crack. My husband is drunk driving with my kids." Because, remember, there are multiple parts of a divorce. Most people don't think about it, but it's true. A divorce is a lawsuit, a legal action. And most of the time they have a child custody component.

Someone calls me on the phone and says, "I want to know exactly what my husband's doing. I want to know who he's doing it with, how often he's doing it, and where he's doing it. Is he doing it that way? Is he doing it this way?"

What I end up telling them is, "Honestly, if you're investing in that because there's something that you need to know to gain a sense of peace, I understand—and it's something that we can attempt to get clarity on the best that we can. But it's a very expensive thing to do."

A private investigator in the state of Texas probably averages around $100 an hour for general surveillance, and it can mount up fast, even when there's a GPS unit on the car, which makes tracking them far less time consuming than it used to be—because the person following the movements doesn't have to be watching every minute. If the husband gets up and goes to work at eight o'clock in the morning, and he works till five o'clock in the afternoon; unless he leaves the office for a period of time, there's really nothing to watch. We put the GPS unit on his car and establish over a few days what his pattern of movement is. Is he going to the office and staying there?

If he's actually having an affair in the office, it's a little difficult to document that from a video perspective. It's not like you can just stroll into someone's private office and say, "Gee, you're having sex on the couch in your office. Let me videotape it." You have to establish some reasonable expectations with the client because oftentimes clients think that when they hire a private investigator, it's like hiring a private, invisible drone to follow someone. We've had cases where people really want to know exactly what the husband (most often) or the wife is doing, and we learn that the guy always goes to this particular bar. You can set up a meeting at the bar, where you get a younger woman investigator to chat the guy up. It's kind of a fidelity check. The investigator sits at the bar, and after thirty or forty minutes says, "Hey. We've had enough to drink. Let's go up to my room," to see if the person's going to fall for it or not. In my line, this kind of trap is called a "honey pot."

But in this particular case, the guy was too high profile. He probably would not have fallen for a honey pot. You wouldn't have found him at a local watering hole, picking up young twenty-something-year-old women. With someone like this, you would think (a) he was either having an affair in his office, (b) he was sourcing prostitutes, or more likely from a scenario like this, (c) he was sourcing a sugar baby online.

So we got the phone's forensic report back and started looking at it. Was he going onto hookup sites like Seeking Arrangements or Ashley Madison? Was he going to SugarDaddy.com? How was this guy procuring his sex? Was he using prostitutes because if so, remember, the courts may view that as a much higher-risk behavior. If he was going out and having sex with prostitutes, then going home to the wife and having sex with her, even if he was using protection, would be considered a high-risk behavior.

Now, because the guy kind of looked like your average alpha male, I really was expecting to see some kind of girlfriend deal or chitchats with his attractive young admin—but that's not what we discovered. It turned out that this guy was into having unprotected sex with transvestites. And he was sourcing the transvestites from really hard-core hookup sites. There was one called Grindr, which targeted gay males, and there were others, too. These weren't dating sites, they were, "Hey. I'm anonymous male X. I'm looking for anonymous male Y." On the Grindr site, you could show pictures of yourself or post a photo of your penis, for instance. In his case, we discovered that he was advertising, "I'm into having sex in bathrooms, through glory holes. And I'm going to be at XYZ restaurant in ten minutes. I want to know if you want to meet me there. Here's how I want it." And he was demanding that the sex be unprotected.

Clearly this guy was into some very high-risk behavior. It was surprising, given how vanilla he appeared, to discover he was into extreme high-risk behavior. It seemed completely out of context with this person's life: this gray-haired, preppy alpha male, driving a nice BMW, living in one of the finer parts of town, involved in all these high-profile charity events. This was not the guy you would have pictured running around town at eleven o'clock in the afternoon looking to have unprotected glory-hole sex with transvestites. It was odd, and that was what was particularly frightening when you read through his deleted-then-recovered text messages, which included photos of the people he was meeting. What he was sourcing were people who would have sex with him without condoms.

In one of my early meetings with his wife, she had admitted to me that they had no sexual contact between them at all, anymore. I said, "Well, it's not that uncommon for people to go through that after a certain period of time in a relationship. Anything else that you could say?"

She said, "Well, a couple weeks ago, we had gone out. I thought we were going to have sex. We were getting along real well. We got into bed. I was kind of ready to go, and he wasn't. I reached around, and I swear he was leaking something from his rectum."

Of course, when I heard that initially, I thought, "Huh. I wonder what that is." But honestly, even someone like me who has seen every imaginable variation of human sexuality would not have guessed it with this guy—at all. But it was all there on his phone.

Our surveillance over a period of about three weeks showed that this guy was engaging in this extremely high-risk behavior on a very regular basis; whatever his other issues, he certainly wasn't suffering from erectile dysfunction. It's a miracle he hadn't given his wife HIV, hepatitis, or you name it. It's easy to pity someone who's so suppressed, but I didn't feel too bad for him, because he was exposing his wife to the potential catastrophic health hazards of his behaviors. She could have ended up a victim of something that she never agreed to participate in.

And we found more: There's a sexualized fantasy world built around pony characters and cartoons that includes males who identify themselves as "Bronies." These are grown-ups who are really, really into this popular pony franchise, who dress up and act out fantasy scenarios and post photos of themselves online. There's a subgroup of Bronies called "Cloppers"—and Cloppers are people that are into truly sexualizing the ponies. They all have "Pony" names, and an attractive gay male sugar baby is called a "Sparkle Pony." We discovered that our client's husband had himself a Sparkle Pony boyfriend, with whom he'd broken up after eight months. I never knew what a Sparkle Pony was beforehand, but when I looked at the guy's phone, I kept seeing, "He's my SP. He's my SP. He's my SP," and I wondered, "What the hell is that?" So we ended up seeing a picture, finally, of one of these pony figures with sparkles, and it was like, "Oh. It's a Sparkle Pony."

Did I mention they had two kids?

It was my unenviable job to reveal all this to his wife. When she came into my office, I said, "We found some stuff. You probably want to sit down," because I could tell that while she was mentally prepared to deal with Susie Sugar Pants and her husband, she was not prepared for glory holes and Sparkle Ponies. I'm not sure anyone could ever be. When I showed her the photos, she threw up.

In the subsequent divorce, she cleaned up; about 75 percent of their assets went to her, millions and millions of dollars, because this guy did not want this stuff coming out in court. It was resolved very, very quickly in mediation.

This is an example of a case that couldn't have been made at all by relying on traditional methods of detection. This is one where the digital trail this guy left was key to uncovering his activities and getting his wife out of the relationship.

Lesson one from this case is that nobody wants to see what's going on under their nose, especially this kind of thing. Some people are eager to overlook things once they have caught a glimpse; in a lot of these cases, the guy has an affair, and they may say, "Well, he has one affair. What difference does it make?" The fact is that humans have a tendency to push the envelope. So you have one affair, and you have a second, and then you have a third. Then you have two at a time. Once you start testing these things out, what's not okay? It's a big assumption to say, "They might do this, but they certainly wouldn't expose me to some kind of STD risk." In my experience, that's not true. When people are out catting around and doing high-risk behaviors, their judgment is pretty horrible. I always tell my clients,

"Listen. I don't want to make you paranoid, but however bad you think it is, it's worse." That always makes people feel better.

Another lesson is that deviant behaviors—and I'll define "deviant" as non-open truths, things that are kept hidden and closed—don't grow prettier over time. They grow uglier, and the behaviors become increasingly sketchy and more risky. If your husband's bisexual or gay and he's living in the closet, that closet's going to grow nastier and moldier and scarier. People end up progressing, amping up the dose like drug addicts. You don't start off shooting heroin; you make your way down that road, and that road leads to riskier behaviors for everybody. We've had cases like this one where the guy ended up dead; he went to a hotel to meet someone he contacted on a hookup site, and it turned out to be a robbery. They hit him in the head, took his money, and killed him.

Overall, it's better to know your significant other's ugliest truths and worst vices, because then at least you can be in vice management and not be a victim of it.

CHAPTER EIGHT

INNOCENCE LOST

When I was a kid, doing something stupid required some real work on my part. But in today's world, stupid is as close as access to the Internet. The gulf between what parents got up to as kids and what their kids are doing today has never been greater.

If I wanted to do something stupid, the geographic range of what I could get myself into was limited to my community and what trouble I could find in those environs. I'd have to go down to the local badass apartment complex and seek trouble out, and I was limited as to what I could find. If there were some ne'er-do-wells hanging out at the local Stop-N-Go, I could go do underage drinking behind the convenience store with them, but I didn't know what was going on behind all of the doors in this apartment complex or behind the doors of the houses in my community.

That's no longer the case; in today's world, you can immediately join in a cybercommunity that provides a virtual portal into what used to be a much more private and restricted life. And the most obvious area in which this impacts kids is sex. When I was growing up, stealing your dad's *Playboy* or your uncle's *Hustler* was usually the extent of the porn available to you. You would have had to go to a porn bookstore to see anything really hard core, and generally those were few and far between, especially in small towns. Today, all it takes is a couple of strokes of the keyboard on your computer, iPad, or smartphone. Even if you're doing innocent research on sexuality or sexual health, what is going to come back is a lot more raw than anything today's adults would have ever seen when we were kids.

To some extent, I think parents know that today. But at another level, I don't think that they are prepared for how much of this is going on with kids—and at ever-younger ages. The advent of mobile technology, and the efficiency of mobile applications and browsers, makes the exploration of the full range of sexuality a lot easier to do.

The case I'm going to describe here is a good example of all that because it shows how a case got out of control because of parents not monitoring their child. You may be okay with the idea of your kid finding out about sex online—but on the other side, there are predators and offenders that are out there lurking, looking for your kids as they're exploring those sorts of things. And the array of information available online isn't exactly the kind of sex you want your kid to see: bestiality, graphic rape porn, all kinds of variations on the theme that your kid can access even without going to a hard-core site. Things a parent would consider *not* okay to look at are now readily explored, and in the last couple of years we've seen a jump in hookup sites that encourage very rapid and random sexual contacts:

sites like Tinder or Grindr or any of the hundreds of variations out there that exist to match strangers up in the sexual marketplace.

Imagine being a fifteen-year-old boy with your hormones raging, your head full of questions about sexuality, and you go from surfing porn on the web to a pop-up ad that offers, "Hook up with this hot young woman now; text her now. She lives a mile and a half from your house." That's a whole different level of risk and exposure, exponentially greater than what we experienced when we were kids, and I think a lot of people really don't even understand how available it is, how tempting it is, or how well engineered the marketing is.

As always, when you're looking at the bad guys, you need to have respect for the adversary, and believe me, the purveyors of sex on the Internet are some of the best, most specific marketers I've ever seen. They can dial into your secret preferences and vices better than you could imagine. So as someone goes through these sites, if there's a tendency to select a particular type of porn, the systems automatically start showing only that type of porn. The display ads, the pop-up ads, the pay-per-click ads also begin to replicate the preference that is being demonstrated. So for a teen or someone in their twenties, or thirties for that matter, it changes the dynamic. Especially for someone with any kind of impulse control problem—or even just your normal person with a couple of drinks in them. And on the other side of that screen are a hell of a lot of perpetrators and offenders, all looking for victims.

What are the odds that my teenage son could come in contact randomly online with a sex offender? The answer is: very high! Because how does he know who this person is? He's going online, and all of a sudden an ad pops up for Tinder, and there's a sexy picture that's captioned, "I am Suzy, hot girl down the street. I live two miles from you. I am twenty-two, and I want to have sex now. The door is open at my apartment, just come in." We deal with cases where that's exactly what someone will do—where people will abandon all common sense and find themselves in someone's apartment, in someone's bed, without ever having physically met this person before. I would encourage anyone who doubts that to go online for two minutes on Tinder or Grindr. It will blow your mind—and these aren't even considered extreme sites. They're talked about on radio. They're written about in the paper. I mean, any person who is active online, sixteen through thirty, already knows about them.

So the question is, as a parent, how do you monitor that kind of stuff? How do you keep your kids safe? The idea when we're raising our kids is to make them aware of stranger danger. You go to the park to play, and Bob the pervert tells you come over and see his puppy—that's stranger danger. The neighbor three doors down who you don't know offers you some cookies—stranger danger. If a coach or if a teacher takes you away from the other kids and starts touching your body—stranger danger—and you need to report it! But how do you identify and help your kids deal with the stranger danger that is not a physical thing; that has a virtual presence, which only becomes real after you've crossed a line and that line is far, far away from the parents? Possibly the line is crossed in an apartment complex across town that you took a bus to, or in a downtown hotel, where the person waiting might be a murderer or a rapist or infected with some incurable sexually transmitted disease? Those are all real issues.

The answer to the question is that there are technologies that are easily installed on kids' mobile devices; things like WebWatcher and mSpy and Net Nanny. Even someone who isn't particularly tech savvy can install these. The software acts as a key logger; this is hacking software that allows you to look at all the text messages and emails that are being sent and received and to look at the websites that are being visited. Kids now use a product called Snapchat that has a feature whereby the text messages and the photos only stay on the phone for a very short period of time until they're viewed, and then they're deleted. If kids want to hide their communications, they'll use Snapchat or one of a whole bunch of different applications that are more Wi-Fi and data-based applications, that don't show a signature on the phone.

If it makes you feel better, discuss the rules openly with your kids when you give them their phone: "Listen, I pay for the phone. There is no expectation of privacy. I may be listening to your phone calls. I may be looking at your text messages. I may be looking at the websites that you're visiting, and the reason I am doing it is because you live in a different world of risk. We talked about stranger danger when you were younger, but the stranger danger today is a digital boogeyman. Just like I would keep an eye on you at the playground, I am going to keep an eye on you online because the online world is a literally near-limitless world, and it doesn't even allow the same sort of geographic checks and balances that I normally would have with you." To allow your kid to go online with absolutely no conditions of supervision is the equivalent of dropping your kid off in the middle of New York City and saying, "Best of luck to you." Keeping an eye on your kid's online activities is not the equivalent of reading your kid's journal. And repeatedly, in cases where the parents have not been vigilant in supervising what their kids are doing online, problem areas come into play.

There are different social sites like Facebook out there that your kids use, and new ones are being developed every day, designed to offer more privacy for the user, regardless of the user's age and apart from parental discretion. A parent should remember, too, that we have a different definition of "friend" than the one our kids have. If someone over thirty says that someone is a friend of theirs, the assumption is that they're talking about a person they physically have met and know. But ask your teens about their friends, and you'll find that their list will include more than a few people they've never actually met; these are virtual relationships, strictly online. Yet your teen may consider this virtual friend to be a close friend, even a confidante. What they don't seem to understand is that their "friends" may not be who they seem to be.

We had a client family whose story was typical. Their daughter was part of a group of girls who were very tight on Facebook. The age range was twelve to fifteen. Some had met at school, some had met at camp, and this collective of girls spent an awful lot of time chatting online with each other on Facebook, sharing photos and updates. What none of them realized was that one of them was a phantom—a lurker who used photos lifted off the Internet to create a false identity as a young girl. The person was good at it, absolutely pitch perfect; the person knew the slang, the references, the mores of this little community, and some of the inside jokes between the girls in the group, so that "she" fit in seamlessly to this little community.

But in this particular case, the phantom "friend" wasn't actually a thirteen-year-old girl. This person was an adult, male, convicted sex offender who had engineered numerous virtual identities on various Facebook pages in an attempt to get one of the girls to come meet him. This fifty-three-year-old registered sex offender had been convicted of a whole host of absolutely heinous crimes. Like most sex offenders, he had a niche that he played in, and his niche was budding, pubescent girls; and young adolescent girls make up one of the most worrisome of all populations that I've ever dealt with, because they're simultaneously the smartest and dumbest group.

The parents came to us when the dad noticed his daughter was withdrawing from normal family and social activities into this obsession with texting on the phone; she had gotten into trouble for texting in class, and she was texting late into the night. But when the dad looked at the cell phone records, nothing showed up, and he couldn't understand that. Then he happened to see that the texting, which had begun on Facebook, was showing up on his daughter's cell phone. The number appeared to be local, but it was in fact a virtual phone number, something you can create with two clicks on your computer—and that allows you to make it look like you're located anywhere you choose.

When the dad called us, he said, "Something's going on, but I don't know what it is. My daughter's acting weird, very erratic, and she's making all these odd requests. She wants to go visit one of her friends from camp in Dallas." When he'd asked her who this friend was, her explanations seemed off-center, not quite right. We told him to get that phone, and bring it to us.

When we finally got possession of the daughter's phone, it was a big to-do, because her parents were worried about violating her privacy. But on my advice, they finally got possession of her phone, and we forensically imaged it, recovering a lot of the text messages that she had deleted. In fact, a lot of those messages had been deleted at the request of the person who was sending them—her virtual "friend".

Over the course of this carefully developed relationship, the daughter had been talked into believing that she and "Sammi" had met briefly at a dance, and their subsequent friendship was entirely online. Going through their communications, it became pretty clear to me pretty quickly that Sammi was not a thirteen- or fourteen-year-old girl. The language, the style of it, the manipulative skills—all of it felt much more mature, and it looked exactly like what an adult would do to try to get a kid to come and meet him out of town.

When we imaged her phone and computer and looked at the Facebook conversations, we saw that this young girl had spent a year chatting with this person and that she had shared all of the intimate details of her life: the disputes with Mom, the disputes with Dad, daily discourse and disputes with the siblings, troubles in school, dreams, hopes, fantasies. In this girl's mind, this was a deep and meaningful relationship; Sammi was now her best friend, and she wanted her parents to fly her up to Dallas to spend a weekend with her. But it was clear to me that it was not a child on the other end but an adult, most likely male, and this person was doing his best to get this girl where he wanted her—away from her parents and into his hands.

When the parents took her phone and computer from her, it was like they were taking heroin away from a junkie. They had to send her to stay with her grandmother, under suicide watch. She had a complete meltdown when we sat her down and told her that her girlfriend Sammi in Dallas didn't exist; that she was a ghost, created by a predator to lure her in; and that the whole gallery of photos—of Sammi and her dog, of Sammi with her family at Disneyland, of Sammi at school—were not actually photos of the person who was posting them. We had to explain that if someone wants to tell you a lie in today's world, the Internet can help that person create an unbelievably thorough lie—and that she had been the victim of a massive lie.

Naturally, she refused to believe it.

So we took over communications. We started communicating with the so-called "Sammi" as the young girl, and we worked with the local police. We had set up an entire sting where we arranged to meet him at the Marriott near the airport, and we worked it all the way down to the room. When the police went in the room to get this guy and searched the room, they found all kinds of bondage gear: handcuffs, ropes, ties, and gags. We think he was actually going to kidnap her. Where it would have gone from there is anyone's guess—but it's likely she wouldn't have been coming home. Subsequent police investigations revealed that he was working three different victims at the same time.

If you're a parent, you need to be aware that the outside world is intruding on your family and on your kids. It's coming in on the Internet. It's being socially manufactured on your kids' friends network. If you don't physically know somebody—and by that I mean you've literally met this person face to face, touched the person, and verified that the person is indeed the same as his or her online persona—do not assume that the whoever it is will be legitimate. In the old days, you wouldn't have let your kid go to someone's house to play if you didn't know the family, right? In today's online world, you've got to adhere to the same standard, and if you don't follow that rule, you risk a lot. You risk letting a predator manipulate your kid, someone who can get to them in ways that are a lot deeper than you can deal with.

It took a long time and a lot of therapy for this girl to recover. First, she was dealing with the emotional loss of someone she'd seen as a best friend. It took three weeks for her to accept and believe that this man had been posing as the "friend" in whom she'd confided so much for so long. She saw that she had knowingly violated all the safety rules that her parents had laid out, but she came to realize that she, too, was a victim. Also that there were some things her parents had never warned her about, because the parents weren't aware of these dangers. These were not private investigators and computer forensic experts. These were just normal people—and they had come dangerously close to actually buying her that ticket to Dallas. Chances are that she'd have disappeared, and they'd never have known what happened.

A good piece of advice that I share with all of my clients is, "Trust but verify"—especially when it comes to your kids. It's not about being hypercontrolling; it's about the responsibility of creating a safe space for your kid to grow and live, and for better or worse, the cyberworld is part of that space now. The problem with it is, it has no fences. There's no access control. It's a free-for-all, with no rules, no limits, and no standards. And you don't want your kid there, in the same way you wouldn't want your kid to go to an open-air concert in the middle of the city at two o'clock in the morning without any supervision.

And the threat isn't just sexual; it's exposure to drugs and worse. Much worse. Did you know there are people online whose kink it is to encourage suicidal kids to kill themselves? Well, now you do. You might think your kid is safe, because you're sure that he or she isn't sending naked selfies to a predator—but every kid gets depressed, every kid has dark times, and there are groups out there ready to capitalize on that. I mean, there are webcams on sites that try to get people to kill themselves while other people are watching it, as they're sexually gratifying themselves. Then they swap the death videos like baseball cards. This is the world we live in. This is the world our children are growing up in. Just because we as parents don't see it doesn't mean that our kids don't.

Honestly, if you knew everything that was out there, waiting for them online, you might just take away your kid's phone permanently. I am not advocating that; I am just saying, realize that this is out there, and put monitoring software on your kid's phone. Use these tools, and make sure you know who your kid's friends really are.

Make sure *they* do, too.

CHAPTER NINE

ENGINEERING
INDUSTRIAL
ESPIONAGE

This story centers on a company that's in the middle of the development of the fracking spaces in Texas. It's slowed down a little bit, but a few years ago a lot of start-up wildcat companies were exploding onto the scene and growing very fast. Many of them, at least in Texas, centered around what they call the Eagle Ford Shale in South Texas. You probably are aware that in Houston especially but also in Dallas, Midland, Odessa, and even San Antonio, there are a large number of energy-services companies centered within that area. They provide oil-field services to the Texas shale markets and the other shale markets developing in the Dakotas and Pennsylvania and even some of the shale fields that were discovered in China and in other parts of the world. Texas is a global center of energy innovation, and a lot of the capital associated with those companies—the private equity groups, the venture-capital groups, the high-net-worth individuals who fund these innovations—come from these parts of Texas. Our client was one of these fast-growth companies involved in the development of what they call fracking sciences, specifically in the machinery that goes into drilling fracking wells.

This company was on what we'd call the J-curve of growth; from start-up to boom; at year one, one million dollars in revenue; the second year, fifteen to twenty million in revenue; and the year after that, fifty to a hundred million. They were hitting these upturns very quickly, bringing together staff very quickly, and, of course, bringing together capital very quickly. The company was going out into the private equity or venture markets and finding the partners and cash needed to handle these rapid upticks. It's the modern day Gold Rush.

Our client was an innovator in certain types of drill bits that specialized in exploiting these fracking spaces—a very specialized, highly competitive and lucrative area.

The call I got came in on a Saturday morning from the company's attorney. He told me they had reason to believe that a group of their employees had either stolen or were planning to steal the company's proprietary designs, along with client lists and other proprietary information. They believed that the employees were in a conspiracy to do this with a couple of key salespeople who had left the company. They had received word from one of their clients that one of their former salespeople had approached them with hints about a "big new offering." Apparently, it was going to be more competitive from a price and service standpoint than what our client was providing. The Dallas-based CEO of the company heard about this and was concerned enough to fly to Houston to investigate it personally, whereupon he'd called me. He was at the closed offices, trying to figure out what could be going on, and we were there with him within the hour.

Our first step clearly had to be forensically imaging the computers of the fifteen to twenty employees. We really didn't know who was involved, and we needed to gather enough digital evidence to determine what was going on from these computers. Unlike a big company like Exxon, this was a loosely cobbled-together entrepreneurial upstart, buying equipment as needed, sharing computers, sharing thumb drives. It was a perfect setup for someone who wanted to take information from the network in a way that would be hard to discover.

While we were imaging the computers, we talked with the CEO. Who were these salespeople who had left the company, and what did he know about where they'd gone or what they were doing? Sometimes a client thinks he or she is totally in the know about what's going on. In my experience, that's rarely true. The client is in a corner office, at another location. The fact is that if you catch someone stealing ten dollars from your pharmacy, they haven't just stolen ten dollars; they've probably stolen close to $100. You just caught them on ten. If, as in this case, you think that you've caught them stealing one design, they've probably stolen ten designs. Because you're emotionally and financially involved, you don't want to think that the problem is as bad as it is, but only rarely do I find the problem is smaller than originally thought. It's typically always worse. And the problem is more endemic than you think it is; it touches more corners. That's why we keep an open mind about who might be involved in this kind of theft; we assume it's everyone until we can analyze data that narrows it down.

In this particular case, we needed to find some things out pretty quickly. First, what had been attached to those computers, and what had been downloaded to them?

If someone is stealing proprietary designs, they somehow have to get them off the computer. Sometimes they'll use thumb drives, sometimes they'll use external hard drives, and sometimes they'll download and then e-mail the files to themselves. They'll pull up their Gmail account or their Yahoo account or their Hotmail account, and then they'll download the attachment, attach it, and finally close out the browser, hoping that there is no evidence that shows that they have sent anything. We're looking for the path of the information leak. How could the data have come off those computers and then removed offsite?

We're also looking at any sort of chatting that the people have done internally. People will download their Yahoo messenger account on their work computer, and they'll be messaging to each other offsite. Alternately, they'll message each other via their cloud e-mail, their web-mail, their Gmail, Yahoo etc. to communicate without using their company e-mail, because they believe that their company e-mail is housed in some sort of Outlook exchange server.

We're also looking at the web history; what are they doing during the day? Are they looking up competitors? Sometimes, they're Googling things like, "How to hide the fact that I'm stealing information at my company". At one of these investigations, we found an employee was investigating how to download information off a computer without being discovered, which to me is a fairly good indicator that the person's up to no good.

In this case, we realized pretty quickly that four of the twelve employees working there were actively communicating and in conspiracy with two of the people who had recently left. A third former employee had started a company when he'd left about eleven months prior. It was unclear how this new company had been financed or what the source of money was, but six months after it was formed, the two salesman left to join it. Now, we began to see a trail indicating that the company engineers were funneling information out to these three people—so all of these guys had broken their non-compete agreements, which precluded them from leaving and starting a new company. Certainly, they weren't supposed to be stealing proprietary information, including lists of clients and pricing to these clients.

When you effectively steal the investment a company had to make in order to win a particular client and to serve their needs, you have unjustly enriched yourself by what was not available in the general market. Say that a small energy-services company was in the process of buying specialized drill bits for a fracking project that they had kept secret and that the particular type of drill bit was going to be a competitive-edge innovation in the market. I never could have known that unless I had been an employee of this company at that moment in time. Whether or not I had a non-compete agreement signed, most courts in United States are going to say that basic civil law prevents me from stealing that information. It's no different than if I had broken into the offices at night and stolen it.

To prevent unscrupulous people from gaining benefits of that kind, companies try to get what are called temporary restraining orders or TROs. To get a TRO, you first have to prove that there is a reason that you should have one. In this case, we worked with the client and attorney to gather enough information to show a court that these people didn't just quit and start a competing company legitimately. They hadn't done their own R&D, created an innovative drill bit, and gone into the marketplace to promote it. What they did was steal our client's information, trying to produce the product cheaper and then selling it back to the existing clients who they already knew—all based on the information they'd stolen from my client.

That's not what free competition is all about. That's intellectual property theft. That's exactly what non-competes are designed to prevent from happening, because if you're allowed to do that freely, it would bring an end to innovation. The entrepreneurs who take on risk and the people who finance those entrepreneurs—in essence the free-market innovation that drives America—would have no protections. All you would do is wait for someone to innovate something and then steal it. That's why the Chinese target us, because they're experts at that. We're experts at innovation; they're experts of replication. What's the real difference between an employee stealing it or an outside entity hacking the network and stealing it?

We were quickly able to assess the information our forensic team had found. When we were done, we installed monitoring software on the key computers—which was perfectly legal, as they were the property of the company. We didn't want them to come in on Monday and be fired; we wanted to monitor them and see what they were up to. Sure enough, on Monday morning, the e-mails and the chatting started up, all about what they were doing: "We need these detailed AutoCAD files with the prototype of our work." They tried to hide what they're doing, even though they'd talked themselves into believing that what they were selling was somehow theirs—because it was really version 2.0 of the original idea. Never mind that they actually created version 1.0 and were paid to do so; they felt that it was their baby, and this CEO didn't really appreciate how handsome and intelligent it was. He was too stupid to "get" the brilliance of version 2.0, so in their eyes, they were its rightful owners. Forget about all the laws, forget the agreements that you signed saying that the stuff you innovate for the company is *property* of the company. In the mind of someone stealing, all of that is inconsequential at that moment in time. We discovered via one of these chats that a couple of the existing engineers would be at an upcoming trade show in Houston, at which the emphasis would be on innovation in the fracking space. Now, it was time to move into traditional investigative mode.

We pulled together background files on all the staff members engaged in stealing from the company, and these files covered the whole profile of who they were. I read through at least a thousand of their emails to get a fix on them: What was driving their desire to harm their company? What was their motivation? The more we knew going in, the easier it would be to draw them in.

We made plans to attend that trade show, posing as this group's perfect client. We developed a background story of being representatives of a family office that was looking to invest in innovations in the fracking space. We registered at the trade show, where these guys would be at our client's booth, ostensibly representing his products. I get my nametag with my fake business name on it, and I'm good to go.

I headed for the company booth, and I intentionally struck up a conversation with one of the guys who I knew was not involved in this scam. I saw that the guy we were targeting was listening in. I turned my attention to him and started talking with him. One of the things that we have to do from a traditional investigative standpoint is become fairly fluent on the topics we're dealing with pretty quickly. So in the days leading up to that tradeshow, I became an expert on the technologies of drill-bit heads, from fracking to normal drills, offshore and onshore. Now I had this guy's full attention, so I said,

"Come have a cup of coffee with me—I don't want take up your valuable time in the booth."

Once I had him apart from the others, I laid it out for him: "Look, this is very innovative, but you should know that I'm here looking for innovative people who have a unique technology that we can back. We have our eyes on you and what you guys are doing at this company, and our perception is they're holding you back."

It's common knowledge that most start-ups are undercapitalized; even if they've raised money, they haven't raised enough money. He bit hard; within thirty-six hours we had a meeting set up with the three guys who had left and the two engineers who were still present in the company. We met them in one of the private back rooms of an exclusive country club, and we had the fruit plates and coffee service set up; all the bells and whistles. We wowed them with the background of what our family office had been involved in and all these investment we had made. They then proceeded to give us their business pitch.

At some point I said, "I'm interested in getting into some details about what you think is innovative about this drill bit"; they told me that they happened to have brought along the brand-new prototype with them. So I sent one of my guys out to go lug it in from their car.

Now, of course we were recording this meeting in the country club from three different locations: via body wires, video, everything. We got phenomenal video and audio of this meeting and them dragging in this seventy-five-pound bit. We got great footage of the engineer disassembling the bit and giving us a section-by-section description of what was innovative about it. It was exactly our client's bit, part by part, from how it was constructed to what made it different. It is stolen intellectual property.

At that point I decided to go out on a ledge because I already had him, stone cold. We already had the forensic information. In addition, I now had a videotape of the guy talking us through the construction of this drill bit that anyone could see was exactly our client's design. So I thought, *Let's push it a little and see how far he'll go.* I said to him, "Listen, we've done our due diligence before coming here. We know where you guys have worked and where you work now. We know that this is something you've worked on for this other company, and we're fine with that, but how are you going to conceal the fact that you've stolen it?"

The guy said, "I don't think that's going to be a problem. Our CEO is a real ADHD airhead." He went on from there, tearing down the boss, and then said, "He'll never care, and we all know that while this may look like his drill, there is something we are going to be adding to the design that's going to make it unique. Plus, ours is going to cost you 40 percent less than he'd charge you, and money matters. So I wouldn't be too concerned about it."

I said, "It's not the first time that I have been involved in a deal where we ripped off someone's design, so if you are not worried about it, I am not worried about it. I'll just lawyer up; I'll out-lawyer the guy."

We left, we checked out our recording—all good. We went to see our client, who was flabbergasted; "Holy shit!" You could have deposed these guys for weeks and not had this.

In this particular case too, the company had given their employees cell phones. This country-club sting took place on a Friday; on Monday, they terminated them all and collected the company cell phones. On their cell phones, we discovered damaging texts back and forth between the perpetrators, not just about their plans to rip off the technology but also things like how they were spending company money at strip clubs.

This is why investigations that combine both the forensic and the traditional models of investigation are so powerful, because you get incontrovertible evidence that will stand up in any court. They got an emergency TPI, transition to a permanent injunction, and meanwhile filed a civil suit against the perpetrators and shut them out of business. They've gotten a huge judgment against them, worth millions and millions of dollars, and that drill bit they were trying to steal is still cutting edge in the marketplace today.

Do not assume that the client has full knowledge of what's going on in a case because it's nearly always worse than it first appears.

It is important to gather as much of the digital evidence as you can and to properly forensically process it so that you can see what's really going on. That includes information from laptops, desktops, servers, email exchange, and smart phones. That information informs how you design the combination of traditional skills and undercover work needed in order to set the most effective trap for your thief. The best evidence in the world is someone admitting his or her own theft. It doesn`t get any better than that. But it's still very, very difficult to get cases like this one to court without help like ours, because the local district attorneys' offices are so unskilled in the issues of intellectual property theft, even in big cities. It almost takes a state-sponsored act for any government agency to get involved.

The only agencies in America that are really prepared to look at that are federal, and the FBI, Secret Service, and Customs have reasonably well-staffed forensic and cyber units. But at the state and local level, not only do they lack the forensic labs and expertise to follow up, but they don't have district attorneys who understand how to prosecute such cases. In their minds, they see them as civil disputes.

Our client ended up getting justice in the civil court because that was the only vehicle available to him. That's a big problem; this company had spent fifteen million dollars over two and a half years in designing this drill bit, and these guys had admittedly stolen it. And that doesn't even take into account what the market value was; that's just their R&D. Yet, because law enforcement is so behind the times, without our help the company would have had no shot at keeping its property and rescuing its investment.

CHAPTER TEN

THE CASE OF THE WORKPLACE PORN FREAK

What do you do when you learn that one of your employees is looking at kiddie porn on his work computer?

When an executive received an anonymous tip that one of his employees was using time at work to look at child pornography, he called us. An important distinction to keep in mind is that child porn is illegal pornography. Illegal pornography covers a wide range of things, not just child pornography but also snuff films or films of rape or assault. If you suspect that there is child pornography or other illegal pornography on a computer that you own or is in your workplace, that triggers a number of different legal issues for you as an employer.

This executive was concerned because he didn't know exactly who was calling and informing him about this or *why* the person was calling and informing him. The person wouldn't give a name but said it had not been reported to the police, which made the executive suspicious. Another red flag for him was that the purported kiddie-porn watcher was in the middle of an ugly, contentious divorce.

So he called us, and we did what we normally do, which is to run our own background check on this employee. We didn't care that the employer had conducted one when he hired the guy, because in our experience those checks aren't particularly comprehensive. Even assuming they did run a decent background check on him, that's only relevant for the time period prior to hiring the person, For instance, if I hired you on March first, and on March fifth you were arrested and you called in sick, how would I know? Even if you had been arrested six months prior to coming to your employment, that judicial information may not have made its way into the stream of databases at the time when I was checking you out. So you really don't know. That information becomes extra-critical when it's implied that there is some kind of criminal activity going on.

If you called me on the phone and said, "I think so-and-so is involved in illegal pornography," the first thing I'm going to do is go online and look in my databases, and— bingo—I'm going to discover that so-and-so is a registered sex offender. Now that claim has more validity than if the person had no record. In cases of illegal pornography, sometimes you find things, and sometimes you don't—so just the fact that they don't have a record doesn't make them innocent; this could just be the first time they've ever been caught.

In this case, the background check turned up zero: nothing criminal, nothing civil, not even a stray parking ticket—only that this guy was in the middle of a divorce. Now, the client we had didn't know this, but the divorce filings were extremely coarse; there were all kinds of allegations being thrown around by both parties alluding to domestic violence and allegations of inappropriate relationships with their child. I mean it was a real mudslinging, old-school nasty divorce, where nobody was going to come out a winner. It was two bucks fighting to the death in the woods, leaving behind nothing but skeletons with locked horns. It was clear to me, reading those divorce papers, that it was *that* kind of thing, and they were spending money they didn't have on this bitter divorce with one kid at stake. But we still had to check.

The employee in question had both a desktop and a laptop computer, and he also had a company-provided iPhone. In order to get all of his gear in, we staged an IT issue with the cooperation of their IT guy, creating a problem on his laptop so he'd bring it in. We also cut off service to his phone, so he'd bring that in, too. We forensically imaged all three devices, processed them, and then started to search them for porn, hidden or otherwise.

You can do this in a couple of different ways. In one way, sometimes people store files on their computer and try to hide the files by encrypting them to try to circumvent anyone being able to find them. But the software that we use is designed specifically to look for that type of information. They're kind of interesting programs; some of them look for skin, for instance. We looked through the guy's computer, and we didn't see anything. We look through his laptop, and again, we didn't really see much. We saw some pornography on there but just your garden variety—nothing illegal.

When we examined his phone, though, we found he'd been visiting porn websites but not illegal ones. We're talking about legal and fairly commonly found websites. There was some very aggressive acted-out pornography on these sites that you might think is illegal, but it's not. It's really actors and actresses staging events, but it involves people holding people down, people choking people: all of which looks like sexual violence. I don't mean like a kind of a "lite" version, à la *50 Shades of Gray*, I mean it looks like someone is actually being sexually assaulted, and it's hard to watch. It would make most people think, *How the hell is this even on a "normal" pornographic site?* and, *What is the market for this?* These sites spell it out that these are actors and that they're all of legal age—although it's clear that they're cast because they look much younger, like fourteen, fifteen, or sixteen years old. We saw some of that on this person's computer. The good news for the employer was we didn't find any evidence that the person was involved in illegal pornography, meaning there weren't images of underage children or anything like that.

On the other hand, this created a unique problem for the employer. This was not a huge company, and they didn't have a written policy about what you could look at or not look at while at work. There were maybe fifty people working there, and most of them had known each other for a long time. They were using Facebook, they were using LinkedIn, and they didn't have restrictions on what they could search on the Internet. It wasn't like working at a Fortune 100 where a lot of that stuff would be filtered or blocked. When I asked the boss, "What would you do if you saw someone looking at *Playboy* or the Internet equivalent at work?" He admitted that while he certainly wouldn't encourage it, neither would he have fired someone for it. But when you're faced with the issue of the person looking at this quasi-violent pornography, what do you do?

We were pretty sure that the source of the tip to search the guy's computer had come from his soon-to-be ex or her operatives, but the boss was, in fact, fairly disturbed by some of the things the guy was looking at. He didn't end up firing the employee, but he did take the opportunity to put a "no porn at work" policy in place, along with some filtering software and restrictions on the work computers.

But it brings up what I'm seeing as an increasingly common issue in these kinds of divorce cases, where one party anonymously makes a radioactive allegation about the other. And the fact is, if someone wants to be really nasty and has a few hundred dollars to spend on hiring a hacker, it would be possible to actually plant child pornography on your computer, and you would never know it was there until a tipster directed the police to search your hidden files. In fact, not only could you plant all kinds of illegal porn on someone's computer, you could easily set it up so that it would send these photos and material to people on the person's mailing list, thus turning him into a disseminator of illegal porn. We have had cases where we believe that's exactly what has happened.

It's very easy for someone with a grudge against you to destroy your life, your career, and your finances with just a few keystrokes. As an employer faced with this kind of issue, I think that it's prudent—before calling local law enforcement or the FBI—to do some due diligence on the allegation and see if it has any merit. Misinformation or disinformation, whether intentional or unintentional, can have extremely dire consequences to the individual against whom an allegation is made and also to the business. This is a good example of how someone avoided that.

Now, if we *do* find evidence of illegal pornography, we're obligated to report that to law enforcement. The reporting obligations are very clear for any kind of private investigator or anyone else for that matter.

We sometimes also work on divorce cases from the defense side. We'll get a call from an aggrieved spouse saying that her soon-to-be ex-husband watches illegal pornography or has a collection of child porn on his computer. It is responsible and reasonable to have a computer-forensic examiner and an investigator check to see if, in fact, that's true and also whether it's possible that it was planted there by somebody else. It shouldn't be the kind of allegation that is not worthy of critical analysis. It is something that can be done to people. It's a crime that can ruin someone's life. So it's not something to be taken lightly. It's certainly not something to be used as an offensive tactic to destroy somebody.

Realize that workers bring personal issues into the workplace all the time, including potentially radioactive personal issues like divorce or child-custody disputes. Just as a domestic dispute can spill over into a workplace violence issue, there can also be a cyber version of that. Plus, you should also realize that people can stumble into actual illegal pornography pretty easily these days.

Do your due diligence. Figure out if there's merit to it. If there is merit, then we can help you bring it to the proper law enforcement. But check it out yourself first, and get help if you need to. There's too much at stake to risk a too-hasty judgment.

IN CLOSING...

None of the cases outlined in this book could have been solved without two discrete sets of skills; the traditional skill set of the private investigator and the computer-forensic skills that allowed us to follow the digital crime trails the perpetrators leave behind. Whether you're in law enforcement or in the private sector, we share the need to get to the truth to cut through the scrum of human distortion, both intentional and unintentional, and arrive at the facts of a matter. That's how the science of criminology evolves out of that need. The digital side of it is nothing more than a continuing extension of tools being used to analyze human behavior and to document and get insights on what humans have done in the process of committing a crime: What did they say? Who did they communicate with? What was their intent? What was their state of mind?

In some ways, the gap between traditional detecting and the new digital methods is a generation gap, where you have people in their late forties and older who just don't have the same comfort level and understanding of how all of this data transforms itself into the cyber world. You would have to go back to the invention of the printing press to find something analogous in terms of the impact the Internet has had on society, and even that pales in comparison.

So when you're working as an investigator, whether it's with the police or in the private sector, and you are a serious practitioner, you have to understand the tools that are available. These tools are evolving at a rapid pace, and as people count more and more on their digital devices to communicate—their cell phones, computers, tablets, etc.—you need to be able to access and analyze that data, or you're severely handicapped. How can you track their movements by using the GPS on their phones? Who are they emailing with, and how are they emailing? Are they texting on their phones? Are they using chat from social media? Are they using texting programs that are designed to not be discoverable that make those texts self-destruct? There's a whole new evolution of technology that's literally designed to hide communication. If all that's occurring, why is it occurring? Is it because someone is trying to hide something?

It's an evolving medium, how investigators use what they find by looking at people's social media. We've made a number of cases and found missing people by going through their social media, for instance. But the sad fact is that very few police departments have anything like the kinds of digital-detecting expertise or technical know-how they'd have needed to solve the cases in this book. At the level of the NSA or the CIA, maybe, but not your local cops—not even in a big city like Houston. And while you may be able to hire a hacker or someone else with those skills, they don't have twenty years of private investigative experience in understanding human behavior, understanding profiling, and understanding all the traditional investigative methods that also have to come into play. You have to have those skills to do an undercover surveillance, to be able to socially engineer an exchange with someone in person, or to get them on a recording admitting to what they've done.

The problem with it all being cyber is exactly that; it's cyber. If I'm not able to take that digital information and simply view it as a data point, the answer that someone has is, "all of that stuff that you found online, that's not me," or, "Yes, that's my Facebook page, but I didn't put that on there. Someone hacked my Facebook page."

And you can't prove otherwise; unless you have a camera sitting on top of someone recording the keystrokes being entered, as well as the corresponding time stamp of the computer showing the information, it is possible that someone else *did* enter that information. Do you know for sure that you have control over your Twitter account at this very moment?

Of course you don't. What if someone hacks your Twitter account and uses it to threaten the president or threatens to kill an ex-lover? There's no way to identify that. Even if I forensically imaged your phone and could see that the text was entered into Twitter at 9:36 this morning, how do I prove that that cell phone was in your hands at that time? Your husband or wife could have done it.

I think what's important is that it's a meaningful data point and that investigators, law enforcement, and private sector people need to fully understand and to keep up to date with. They need to understand the evolution of what it means in real time. We have to dedicate the time and resources and effort to keep up with this ever-shifting digital landscape, while understanding that it's not a be-all and end-all. There will always be a place for the traditional investigator's skills, for the guy who can go in the field and deal with the human element of an investigation. However, it's a combination of these two skill sets that make us nimble enough to be able to combat the evolving threat of our real adversaries: criminals and other people who mean this nation harm.

A recent case in which a major league baseball player called on the Internet hacker world to help him uncover some cyberbullies threatening his daughter raises more than a few ethical and moral questions. Is this how we're going to handle such threats? Will this evolve into an offensive structure? We're doing it as a nation, with cyberattacks on hostile governments, who are in turn doing the same thing to us. When someone slanders you online, as in this case, do you actively find out who it is and then crash his or her accounts? The reason this ballplayer took matters into his own hands was because law enforcement wasn't going to do anything about that. If you called law enforcement and said, "Someone threatened to kill me on Facebook," they wouldn't know what to do with that. I hear this all day long; people call the police because they're being threatened on social media, but the cops don't have the skills, and they don't have the technicians, so they don't have a starting point.

Kids carry out their whole lives on social media. If you were running the police force for the Chicago public schools, and you don't have the full computer-forensic capability to be able to image someone's phone, how would you stop the next school shooter? If you look at kids' cell phone bills today, they don't "speak" to anybody. It's all texts. I guarantee you, the next Columbine shooters are texting each other. If you tried to investigate such a threat right now without a readily deployable mobile-forensic system, what would you do? Would you try to get a wiretap for their phones? For what? They don't speak on the phone. The last people they still talk with on the phone are their parents—and they even try to avoid that.

All we can do as investigators is to work at evolving quickly enough to keep up with the bad guys and hope that, eventually, law enforcement catches up. Until they do, we'll go on handling bad.

If you would like to reach me, please email me at dweiss@mccanninvestigations.com.

9 781599 325910